MW00561407

The
Natural Family
Where It Belongs

The
Natural Family
Where It Belongs

NEW
AGRARIAN
ESSAYS

ALLAN C. CARLSON

Transaction Publishers
New Brunswick (U.S.A.) and London (U.K.)

Copyright © 2014 by Transaction Publishers, New Brunswick, New Jersey.

All rights reserved under International and Pan-American Copyright Conventions. No part of this book may be reproduced or transmitted in any form or by any means, electronic or mechanical, including photocopy, recording, or any information storage and retrieval system, without prior permission in writing from the publisher. All inquiries should be addressed to Transaction Publishers, 10 Corporate Place South, Piscataway, New Jersey 08854-8042. www.transactionpub.com

This book is printed on acid-free paper that meets the American National Standard for Permanence of Paper for Printed Library Materials.

Library of Congress Catalog Number: 2013012446
ISBN: 978-1-4128-5284-5
Printed in the United States of America

Library of Congress Cataloging-in-Publication Data

Carlson, Allan C.
  The natural family where it belongs: new agrarian essays / Allan C. Carlson.
        pages cm
  1. Families—United States. 2. Rural families—United States. 3. Country life—United States. 4. Sociology, Rural—United States. I. Title.
  HQ536.C374 2013
  306.850973—dc23

                                                  2013012446

To the memory and legacy of Pitirim Sorokin and
Carle Zimmerman

Contents

Foreword:
"Agrarian Fairy Tales"

In his book, *The Outline of Sanity*, G. K. Chesterton remarks that "It is true that I believe in fairy tales—in the sense that I marvel so much at what does exist that I am readier to admit *what might*." He goes on to describe a fairy tale of his own imagination: the recreation in early twentieth century England of a *peasant class*, a rural society composed of happy families residing and working on their own small plots of land and sustained by a vital rural culture.[1]

If already a fairy tale in the England of 1926, such enthusiasm for agrarian ideals may seem an almost pathological vision for early twenty-first century America. All the same, the agrarian prospect was ably summarized in a relatively recent essay by the English anthropologist Hugh Brody:

> A family is busy in the countryside. Mother is making bread, churning butter, attending to hens and ducks that live in the yards and pens beside the house, preparing food for everyone. Father is in the fields, ploughing the soil, cutting wood, fixing walls, providing sustenance. Children explore and play and help and sit at the family table. Grandma or Grandpa sits in a chair by the fire. Every day is long and filled with the activities of this family. And the activities are contained, given purpose and comfort, by a piece of countryside at the centre of which is home. . . . *The family in its farm is the family where it belongs.*[2]

This volume holds to the remarkable thesis that *agrarianism* is alive in twenty-first century America and—if not exactly well—showing clear and enticing prospects for the future. It also emphasizes the evident bond of the healthy, natural family to an agrarian—or agrarian-like—household, where the "sexual" and the "economic" are merged through marriage and child-bearing and where the family is defined in considerable measure by its material efforts. The common thesis is that family renewal will *only* occur as these bonds and goals are recreated and strengthened in the years and decades ahead.

The vision behind this book can be easily compressed: These chapters look toward a landscape of family homes, gardens, and small farm-steads busy with useful tasks and energized by the laughter of many children. They see parents as the primary educators of their young. They celebrate homesteads engaged in the care of young, aged, and infirmed family members. They point to the recreation, in new forms, of a family-centered economy. And they portend a renewal of the true democracy dreamed of by George Washington, John Adams, and Thomas Jefferson.

This book has four parts. In the first part, I describe "The Natural Family at Home." It provides, in effect, an anthropology of this type of household, which distinguishes it from other forms of human cohabitation. While presenting an "ideal type" of agrarian life, this description rests on the premises that the natural family is real, universal in terms of possibility, and rooted in human nature. These truths rest in turn on the testimony from both history and the social, biological, and psychological sciences.[3]

The second part examines twentieth century "Displacements" from this normative order. New economic, ideological, and political pressures left the natural family alienated from its true home. Chapters examine the specific effects of industrial capitalism, gender ideology, and war. The human costs of these changes proved to be vast.

Representative "Dissents" from this transformation find expression in the third part. The voices identified here varied in discipline: some wrote in the language of literature and poetry; others used the constructs of economics. They shared sentiments of grief over the loss of a humane order and anger toward those who willed such a change. In these ways, they resembled prophets.

In the fourth and final part, I describe "Movements Home": the rebirth of family-centered habitation; the reassertion of a "gendered" order; and the remarkable return of family-scale agriculture. These changes suggest that the twenty-first century shall witness renewal of the natural family on the places where it belongs.

Notes

1.   G. K. Chesterton, *The Outline of Sanity* (Norfolk, VA: IHS Press, 2001), 29–30, 34, 70.

2.   Hugh Brody, "Nomads and Settlers," in *Town and Country*, ed. Anthony Bar-
      nett and Roger Scruton (London: Vintage, 1999), 1–2 (emphasis added).
3.   Evidence supporting this statement can be found in: Allan Carlson and
      Paul Mero, *The Natural Family: Bulwark of Liberty* (New Brunswick, NJ:
      Transaction, 2008), Chapters 4–6.

The Natural Family at Home

The natural family rests on submission to the divine spirit and will. These are manifested in human nature and in the broader order of creation. All social constructs strive for harmony with divine intent.

The first and most crucial social bond is marriage. Marriage holds this distinction for it is natural and self-renewing, rooted in the mutual attraction of man to woman, both of whom feel their incompleteness when existing alone. They come together, of necessity, so that the human species might continue. Most cultures place marriage at or near the center of elaborate religious ritual, but the marital institution can be found even among tribal, animist societies, testifying to its universality.

In this sense, marriage is the only true anarchist institution. That is, it exists prior to other human bonds, be they village, city, state, or nation, and it has the endless capacity for renewal, even in periods of persecution, social decline, or moral degradation. In the modern age, each new marriage is an affirmation of life, of love (real or potential), and of continuity against the darkness which threatens to overwhelm the human spirit. Every new marriage is an act of rebellion against ambitious political and ideological powers that would reduce human activity to their purposes. And each real marriage contains within it the power of biological reproduction, a throw of the genetic dice that brings to life new human beings, unique and unpredictable in their qualities.

Marriage bears a special power, as well. Equal in dignity before their Creator, man and woman each hold special gifts, profound and powerful differences in thought, action, and skills. This complementarity transforms their union into something far greater than the sum of its parts.

At the same time, marriage forms the foundation on which humans build other social bonds. Marriage is, at one level, a covenant between two individuals, a man and a woman who agree to give each other mutual care, respect, and protection, and who open their future to the life issuing from their sexual union. Marriage can fulfill this role, and function properly, only when the bond is assumed to be for life. Without that mutual promise, the efforts toward forming "one flesh" of man and woman remain tentative. The marital partners, out of fear for the future, will withhold some part of their investment of time and energy into the marriage. The promise of indissolubility alone encourages the man and woman to negotiate their way through the great differences between them in mind and body and to bring some resolution to their common life. Incompleteness in the promise operates as would a crack in the foundation of a great building, spreading with the passage of time.

Each marriage is also a covenant between the couple and their kin. In marriage, two families merge in a manner that perpetuates and invigorates both. Even in the denatured societies of the modern West, family members will travel great distances to attend the wedding of a cousin, nephew, or niece, still recognizing through residual instinct the importance of both the promise and the event to their own identity and continuity.

More broadly, marriage is the solution to human society's universal dependency problem. Every community must resolve the same issue: who will care for the very young, the very old, the weak, and the infirm? How shall the rewards given to productive adults be shared with those who are not or cannot be productive? In the natural human order, these tasks fall on kin networks, where spouses care for each other "in sickness or in health," where parents nurture, train, and protect their offspring until they are able to create marriages of their own, where the aged enjoy care, purpose, and respect around the hearth of their grown children, and where kin ensure that no family member falls through the family's safety net. Acceptance of these duties passes from generation to generation, as each child views the treatment bestowed by his parents on his grandparents, great aunts and uncles, and so on. These observations teach children, as well, the duty and necessity of begetting their own children, so that the chain of obligation within a family might not be broken.

Marriage is also a covenant between the couple and the broader community. Procreation within marriage offers the best promise of new community members who will be supported and trained by parents without being a charge on others and who will grow into responsible adults able to contribute to the community's well-being.

Predictably, children reared within marriage will be healthier, brighter, harder working, and more honest, dutiful, and cooperative than those raised in other settings. They will be more likely to acquire useful skills and knowledge and less likely to slide into violent, abusive, or self-destructive behaviors.

As such, each true marriage represents the renewal of a community, through the promise of responsible new members to come, which is why every healthy human society invests so much ceremony and rhetoric in the event, and why an array of informal pressures strive to hold the marriage together. These are symbols to the husband and wife of the solemn importance that this event holds to neighbors beyond their intimate relationship and kin. Humans instinctively understand that the strength of their community is dependent, in the end, on the strength of their marriages. If the marital institution weakens—or worse, if it is politicized and subordinated to ideology—then the social pathologies of suicide, crime, abuse, poor health, and crippling dependency surely follow. If continued over several generations, these pathologies born from the decay of wedlock will consume the community itself.

Marriage, in turn, creates a new household. When gathered together, these form the second institutional tier in natural social life, and the one on which all political life is built. The household will normally encompass the wedded man and woman, their children, and aged or unmarried relatives. Successful households are the natural reservoir of liberty. They aim at autonomy or independence, enabling their members to resist oppression, survive economic, social, and political turbulence, and renew the world after troubles have passed. Complete households must have the power to shelter, feed, and clothe their members in the absence of both state and corporate largesse. Such independence from outside agency is the true mark of liberty, making possible in turn the self-government of communities. Households functionally dependent on wages, benefits, and services provided by an outside agency or the state have surrendered a significant portion of their natural liberty, and have accepted a kind of dependency indistinguishable, at its roots, from servanthood. Independence requires that responsible adults in a household be able to forego these forms of support, if necessary, and still be able to ensure the survival of themselves and other household members.

The basic human need for functional independence in food, clothing, and shelter dictates the eternal importance both of a household's bond to property in land and of husbandry skills. Full autonomy requires the capacity to produce a regular supply of food, and the ability to preserve a substantial share of this bounty for consumption during the adverse seasons. The keeping of grazing and meat-producing animals, supplemented by hunting and fishing, adds further to the independence of households and their ability to survive wars, famines, stock market crashes, depression, inflation, and bad government. In arable climates, intensive cultivation of even a few acres of land can provide the necessary bounty that delivers such autonomy; ten to a hundred acres of soil and timber offer an independence more sure and complete.

Accordingly, the natural society views the home and arable land as different-in-kind from other commodities. The most critical of social, political, and economic tasks becomes the appropriate partition, distribution, and use of such property, where ownership is spread as widely as possible, and where freedom of use is conditioned by a responsible stewardship toward future generations.

Together with land, the autonomous household also needs control over the means of production. The industrial revolution of the eighteenth and nineteenth centuries, dependent on balky power sources such as flowing water and the steam engine, gave a monopoly on power to centralized factories, and stimulated the "great divorce" of work from home. For millennia, the great majority had lived and worked in the same place; be it the small farm, the artisan's shop, or the fisherman's cottage. Industrialism severed this bond. This shattered in turn the traditional order of the family farm and village.

The twentieth century, however, did deliver successive waves of new technologies which potentially returned "power," in both senses of that word, to the household economy. Innovations included small electric generators and motors, the internal combustion engine, and the photovoltaic cell. Each of these allows the household to apply power to productive work in the homestead. The household computer is another remarkable new tool once confined to large central work units, but now available for decentralized use. Where the competitive advantage in the nineteenth century clearly lay with the industrial factory, the homestead has improved prospects in the early twenty-first century. Remaining apparent disadvantages often derive from marketing and distributive manipulations that distort real price, or from the corruption of the marketplace by powerful interests.

Rejecting an extreme division-of-labor, natural society also focuses on generalized skill, and the well-rounded human life. It celebrates and rewards craftsmanship, the creative application of human intellect to the fashioning of useful devices. It encourages a form of self-sufficiency.

Young people should learn the basic skills of husbandry and house-wifery: carpentry, gardening, animal care, the preparation and preservation of food, fabric and clothing production. Every strong household also needs to be equipped with ownership of basic tools: the implements needed to grow food; the utensils to process and store produce; the hand and power tools necessary to build and repair shelter and to make clothing; and the transportation vehicles, communication devices, and information storage and processing units necessary to engage in the world of commerce.

In addition, a functional household requires an authority structure, where a responsible patriarchy operates, where family members defer to the wisdom of elders, and where children defer to the guidance of parents. In the healthy civic order, all other loyalties are subordinated to or mediated through this household structure.

A central function of the household is the education of children, for which parents, supplemented by extended kin, are responsible. The household bears the obligation and natural power to transmit to children the spiritual doctrines and beliefs of the family, the customs and folkways by which the household lives, the practical skills necessary for the later creation and sustenance of new households, and the knowledge required for successful engagement in the world of commerce. While outside agencies, such as parent-controlled schools, may be usefully employed for many of these tasks, those households fail which fully abdicate the education of children to others. The education of children, properly engaged, must remain home-centered, where parents impart their visions, values, virtues, and skills to the new generation.

Relative to the world, each household exists as a small collective, organized on the principle of altruism. The members of a household share with each other on the basis of love, without any accounting of individual gain or loss. Under some circumstances, this same principle of justice may extend to other kin, or even to small communities, where the generosity and altruism can be tempered by a practical knowledge of individual character and the discipline which a tight-knit community can bring to bear on its members. This form of small scale organization may exact a price through some loss of efficiency, but it more than recovers this cost through the emotional rewards that household and community life bring.

Indeed, the village, town, or neighborhood, forms the next—or Third—layer of order. A broad society of households allows for the diversification and specialization of skills, within a context of general competence and an expectation of fair exchange. Such collectives operate best when bonded by other affections: a common religious faith; a shared ethnicity; a binding sense of history; the intermingling of a relatively small number of kin groups. Within such communities, the individual internalizes restraints on behavior and ambition, recognizing the threat posed by any form of abrupt innovation. In this level of civic order, children receive a kind of communal rearing, where the sharp edges or peculiarities found in each household can be tempered. Such close community also offers the only effective protection of individuals from pathologies (such as abuse) within households, allowing social intervention to occur without threatening the normative pattern of family living. The village or neighborhood imparts to the young the duties which constitute membership in a community, and models of behavior and rectitude beyond those found in one's immediate household. Public actions are guided most commonly by custom and convention, with formal law generally aimed at the regulation of the stranger. When deviance from community norms occurs, informal and non-aggressive measures such as shunning are normally effective in restoring order and bringing the wayward back into harmony with the community.

Leadership at this level of society emerges spontaneously, as persons living in close proximity to each other easily come to recognize the character strengths and weaknesses of their neighbors, and accept the guidance and wisdom of persons who ably practice both self- and household-governance. They give deference, as well, to the experience of age, a kind of public memory that carries a record of past successes and errors. This natural leadership may be formalized through councils of elders or trustees, or it may be implemented through democratic means. In either case, the leaders accept the great responsibility of protecting their neighbors from internal or external threats that would subvert the bonds of community. Organized community militias, composed of those who study "the arts of war," provide defense against open aggression or gross challenges to public safety. The more complex dangers lie in alien ideologies and technologies that would strike at the heart of healthy community life. Community leaders properly judge such ideologies and technologies, and seek to prohibit or restrict those which would damage the basis of community life.

Commerce occurs between households, through markets. Communities rely on sentiments of common humanity to soften the rough edges of competition, to ensure principles of fair exchange, and to preserve the household basis of the economy. Communities strive to forestall a complete industrialization of human economic and social life. The labor of family members, including in appropriate cases that of children, normally occurs within the family enterprise. Some family enterprises grow larger without losing their family character. When employment outside the household develops, customary arrangements control the corrosive effects of competitive wages by limiting such industrial labor to only one household member and by expecting a family-sustaining wage in return.

Social life at this level also depends on the attachment of individuals to the landscape in which they grow, live, and act, and to the flora and fauna of their native place. Actions such as walking, fishing, hunting, and gardening secure this bond, creating affection for the physical and biological environment which has, in a way, also given life to the individual. This grounding in a small niche of the natural world is vital to the full development of the human personality, and necessary to the attachments which define and hold households and communities together. Deep affection for a place is normally the product of growing up there, whether it be the lake country of Michigan or the soaring mountains of Switzerland. Persons without this sense of native place are left incomplete. They often become perpetual nomads, given to grand visions and ideological constructs designed to fill the emptiness in their hearts.

The next—or Fourth—tier of society is the state. It exists to protect villages, households, and their members from external threat, and to mediate disputes between households and communities that cannot be resolved at a lower level. Having no fixed metaphysic, the structure of the state can vary from place to place, and circumstance to circumstance. The sole guiding principle is the limitation of its power. Natural authority resides in households and communities, where it is conditioned by innate human affections. These entities cede to the state only the minimum power necessary to keep foreign armies and other alien pressures at bay. Constitutional arrangements need insure, as far as possible, that most authority remain in local and household hands, that power granted to the state remain strictly limited, and that leaders of the state be persons of character and self-restraint. Full citizenship in the state is granted only to those who fulfill certain duties:

participation in the common defense through membership in the militia; maintenance of personal independence through a productive homestead; ownership of home, land, and tools; marriage, procreation, and acknowledgment of responsibility for the next generation; and acceptance by one's neighbors.

Natural family order has existed within monarchies, oligarchies, and republics. Monarchical organization has the important symbolic claim of providing leadership of a society of family households by a family. Oligarchies and republics have the ability to draw from a wider pool of talent and virtue. Republics resting on widely distributed small property constitute true democracy. All three forms of traditionalist governance rely on property owners committed to constitutional duty.

The great danger posed by the state is its propensity to become an end in itself, exercising authority not ceded by the foundational social units, but rather claimed as right. Working to destroy the natural order, this rogue state will assert power to "protect" individuals from the rooted authority of households and communities. It will build "state schools" to impart a state morality. It will create artificial "rights" that bludgeon traditional authority. At its most perverse, this wayward state will set wife against husband, husband against wife, children against parents, and household against household. Aggrandizing its own power, this state will weaken the institution of marriage, subsidize sole parenting and divorce, seize the dependency functions of care for the young, the old, and the infirm, transfer the concept of "autonomy" from the household to the individual, and invert the meaning of liberty, casting it as the gift of the state. Such actions destroy natural society, and erect in its place an order where all individuals become—in practice—wards of the Leviathan state. An order of free men becomes a "client society," where bureaucrats minister to the needs of "citizen subjects." Such arrangements invariably bring economic and social decline, since they rest on abstract or imaginary "rights" that are divorced from a sense of duty and from the authentic human affections toward kin and neighbors. Moreover, human "needs" cast under the rubric of "rights" have no natural endpoint, and the effort to meet them through social agency will ultimately consume the wealth of a people.

The last—or Fifth—social tier is the nation. It rests on common-alities that transcend households, communities, and states, among them religious belief, a common morality, language, a shared history, a common ecosystem, inherited folkways, and blood. The conscious-ness of nationhood may wax or wane, encouraged at times by rallying voices who remind a people of "their common destiny," discouraged at other times by voices urging "universal brotherhood" or the creation of transnational "empire," or even forgotten during periods of social and political chaos.

"Nation" and "state" are never found in perfect unity. The whims of history, jealousy, and chance prevent such an ordering. Yet danger lies in even an incomplete merging of these two social tiers, for such a bond inevitably augments the state's claims against family households and communities, by appealing to "the needs of the nation" in a quest for taxes, conscripts, and territory. A sense of nationhood, while necessary to a complete or full social life, is properly mediated through the foundational tiers of state, community, and household, and is often relabeled patriotism. Any attempt by large numbers of individuals to swear first loyalty to the nation, or by the nation to sweep aside the social structures lying between it and the individual, must bring in its wake another form of crisis.

The wild card in human social relations is the corporation, seen here as an artificial, voluntary union of persons toward some common end. This purpose may be religious (as in a medieval monastic corporation), economic (as in the modern multi-national corporation), or intellectual (as in academies of sciences). The common characteristic of the corporation is the manner in which it transcends the natural social constructs of family, community, state, and nation, by claiming the direct and primal loyalty of individuals. Persons joining the corporation weaken, or in some cases even abandon their bonds to the tiers of a natural family order, accepting a new master.

So understood, corporations appear to have existed in most historical ages. Whether its task be missionary conversion to a faith or the production and sale of a commodity, the corporation is part of the human experience. It serves as an agent-of-change, disrupting inherited ways, and reordering the context in which natural society operates. Where natural society tends toward stability, each corporation represents a push for instability, for what Joseph Schumpeter called "Creative Destruction." Conflict between these social visions is inevitable. If the challenge by the corporation is too great, the result can be the distortion or destruction of inherited social life. At the same time, though, the corporation can indirectly help renew natural society, by providing a positive response to challenges. While traditional society can suppress corporate-induced change to the point of stagnation and decline, natural society can also tame, or humanize the explosive force of innovation, turning it to constructive ends. The great test facing any age is to find a workable balance between the satisfactions of continuity through community and the disruptions spawned by corporate-driven change.

The foes of natural society understand that order and liberty rest on this pyramid of relationships: a submission to the sacred; the creation of marriages which flow into households; and the formation of households into communities, states, and nations. While ready to twist or subvert any of these tiers of society, they probably vent their greatest fury against the institution of marriage, for it is on this pillar that all else rests. Accordingly, defense of the sacred canopy and of the marital covenant becomes the moral and political imperative. When they thrive, all else tends to follow, and human existence knows a certain joy and peace.

Displacements

1

Creative Destruction: Family Style

In the wake of Communism's late twentieth century rout by a victorious market capitalism, the pessimistic prognostications of economist Joseph Schumpeter attract less attention. While not a Marxist himself, Schumpeter did adapt some of his arguments from Karl Marx, particularly the view of capitalism as an evolutionary system, one full of nervous energy, one that could "never be stationery." Driving this industrial mutation was the process of "Creative Destruction," which "incessantly revolutionizes the economic structure from within, incessantly destroying the old one, incessantly creating a new one." He emphasized that this "gale of Creative Destruction" did not arise from changes such as new competitors, or price fluctuations, or the flow of the business cycle. Rather, the impulse came from the introduction of new consumer goods, new technologies, new modes of production or transportation, new markets, new forms of industrial organization, or new methods of retailing (e.g., the Walmart triumph over the shops on Main Street). Such changes commanded "a decisive cost or quality advantage" and struck "not at the margins and the outputs of the existing firms but at their ... very lives." In every specific economic field, he wrote, this process left "a history of revolutions" and the debris of ruined companies that could not keep up.

More controversially, Schumpeter also believed that entrepreneurial capitalism could *not* survive. As he formulated this thesis in his 1942 volume, *Capitalism, Socialism, and Democracy*, capitalism's "very success undermines the social institutions which protect it, and 'inevitably' creates conditions in which it will not be able to live and which strongly point to socialism as the heir apparent." He argued that the bureaucratization of large industrial units ousted the entrepreneur, which in turn undid the bourgeoisie as a social class and undermined the very nature of private property. More fundamentally, capitalism

3

leveled the institutions of the preindustrial world: the class of artisans operating through guilds; the village; the agrarian peasantry; and—most notably—the family itself.

Observing data from the 1930s, Schumpeter concluded that marriage, family life, and parenthood meant less to the men and women of modern capitalist societies than they had before. He pointed specifically to tumbling marital birthrates, "the proportion of marriages that produce no children or only one child," as the clearest sign of this revolution in values. It derived from capitalism's "rationalization of everything in life," the embrace by moderns of an "inarticulate system of cost accounting" that exposed "the heavy personal sacrifices that family ties and especially parenthood entail under modern conditions." This "decline of philoprogenitivity," in turn, left homes and home life with less recognizable value. And as "family, wife and children" faded as figures of motivation for the businessman, "we have a different kind of *homo economicus*," one who had lost "the only sort of romance and heroism" that was left "in the unromantic and unheroic civilization of capitalism." As the process undermined the "props . . . of extra-capitalist material" and the "behaviors" on which it rested, capitalism turned toward self-destruction: the passing of entrepreneurship and family-held firms and the "emergence of socialist civilization."[1]

It is on these points that Schumpeter today is faulted. For has not market capitalism triumphed around the globe? Even in once-Communist strongholds such as the Union of Soviet Socialist Republics and the People's Republic of China, do not entrepreneurs rule effectively? Is not socialism in broad retreat, found today only in crude backwaters like Cuba and North Korea?

The problem with these rejoinders is that Schumpeter was quite clear that there were different *forms* of socialism. And it was not the Russian Communist version that he thought most likely to triumph in Western Europe and America. Rather, he pointed to Swedish socialism as the more viable and adaptable model.

What were—and are—its characteristics? Sweden's Social Democrats resolved in the late 1920s to forego most expropriation or nationalization of industry and private property. Let the capitalists remain as formal owners, they reasoned. Instead, the keys would be a close regulation of industry and commerce to achieve social ends, a form of central economic planning through new mechanisms of coordination (e.g., industrial wages would be fixed at a regular meeting of industrial and labor leaders at a seaside resort), and expansion of the welfare state into "The People's Home." Relative to families, this required the socialization of remaining family functions such as early child care and the provision of clothing and meals. Most importantly, said Alva Myrdal, an influential social theorist in the 1930s, labor union socialism itself must change. The goal of "a living family wage" for fathers as heads-of-households must go, as must its companion institution, the "housewife." They would be replaced by a commitment to the absolute *equality* of men and women. In the new order, Myrdal explained, *both* of the genders would be expected to work outside the home. Marriage and home life would be strictly focused on sex and reproduction; everything else would be the responsibility of private industry or government, now informally merged into a vast corporate state.[2]

This union of individualistic or equity feminism with democratic socialism was a historically strange brew. It was hostile to century-old goals of the conventional labor movement, including "the equality of households," "family autonomy," the "family wage," and "the special protection of women and children." And it was not fully realized, even in Sweden, during the 1930s. But three decades later, in the 1960s, its time finally came. It was *this socialism*, with a vision of union between "big business" and "big government" built on the ruins of families and small communities, that would triumph in developed nations around the globe. Indeed, its success would be so pervasive, and its details so distracting, that hardly anyone would even notice the apotheosis of the grand feminist-capitalist-socialist cause.

How, then, might Schumpeter's argument be reformulated or updated to explain this victory? He would emphasize, I think, that the capitalist mindset is imperialistic. It cannot leave anything or relationship untouched. It tends to progressively subordinate other spontaneous communities, such as families and nature itself, to its own values. It injects its peculiar biases—rationalism, cost accounting, efficiency, and consumerism—into precapitalist natural institutions such as families, and so transforms them into very different things. This is creative destruction literally brought home.

The new capitalist economic order and the welfare state grow together. Each picks up functions from the ever-diminishing family household. Business starts by taking over the production of clothes and shoes; it ends by absorbing family meals (e.g., Fast Food) and home cleaning (e.g., Merry Maids). The government begins by acquiring education and claiming child protection; it ends by giving *care* to all who cannot work: the elderly; the sick; preschool children; and even newborns.

In this order, we also need a fresh understanding of that awkward term, *proletarianization*. Marx had defined it as the process whereby workers lost all productive property or capital, coming to rely entirely on wages for their support. Contemporary *proletarianization* might be defined as the steady elimination of independent sources of household income other than wages and the "redistributed" wages of state transfers, where economic gains from "commons" rights, informal economic activity, household production, and other forms of nonmarket work are displaced by industrially organized labor, commercially produced goods, and public welfare. Most western families in the late nineteenth and early twentieth centuries struggled to avoid this loss of liberty, this descent into dependency. But with only scattered exceptions, twenty-first century households in Europe and America have, willy-nilly, already become part of this new order.

While none of the authors openly intended it, evidence for the truth of this neo-Schumpeterian argument can be found in a string of books issued at the recent turn of the millennium on the mounting conflict between work and family. Four of these embrace a common project: to achieve a better mesh or coordination between workplace and home life. But a more accurate description of their joint goal would be to complete, once and for all, the subordination of families to the industrial principle.

Jody Heymann's *The Widening Gap: Why America's Working Families Are in Jeopardy and What Can Be Done About It* is at one level a fairly honest argument for full family surrender to industrialism.[3] She correctly notes that before 1850, most American children grew up in farm families where both parents, in a sense, worked at home. Thirty years later, the rise of industry created a new situation, where the majority of children grew up in families where the father earned a "family wage" outside the home, while the mother labored in the household. By 1990, however, over 70 percent of American children lived in households where both parents were in the industrialized labor force. While glossing over important issues of timing, Heymann does accurately conclude that these changes "were the result *not* of women entering the wage and salary sector but rather of *both* men and women entering the industrial . . . labor force. The fact that both men and women labor is not new. What has been altered radically over the past 150 years for both men and women is the location and conditions of work."

In assessing the consequences of this change, Heymann's working group at Harvard University conducted detailed interviews with 7,500 "working families." With most able-bodied adults at work, they found a troubling new "care-giving deficit." As the author explains: "Whether the issue is elder care or child care, the experiences of low-income families are sounding early, grim warnings for the nation as a whole." The solution, she insists, is certainly *not* to bring the women home. Rather, a program to address "the daily care needs of all Americans" must rest on "the precepts of equal opportunity and equal access."

This means that all able-bodied adults must work, and all nonworking dependents must receive gender-neutral care through "society," meaning—of course—the state. Heymann calls for early childhood care and education for preschoolers by the government on a scale equal to that provided for five- to eighteen-year olds. For those older children, both the school day and year should also be greatly expanded (suggesting that babysitting and adolescent-confinement are displacing learning and acculturation as the driving forces behind the public schools). She also calls for mandatory paid parental leave insurance for all working adults, government subsidies for elder care "community centers," publicly funded child care, and more publicly funded transportation, so that family members can travel with greater efficiency between their various care centers. The Social Democracies of Europe, she insists, have made their peace with industrial necessity (e.g., 95 percent of Belgian three-year-olds are in publicly funded child care centers); so must America.

Giving more complete attention to the revolutionary nature of the new corporate state is Stewart Friedman and Jeffrey Greenhaus' *Work and Family: Allies or Enemies?*[4] The authors are professors of management at the Wharton School of the University of Pennsylvania and Drexel University, respectively. Their list of consultancies is also impressive. Friedman, for example, serves as director of the Leadership Development Center at Ford Motor Company.

In dissecting "the conflict between work and family," the authors focus almost exclusively on *gender*. The point is made over and again: "To create options that help make allies of work and family . . . we need to change the traditional gender roles" (p. 15); "Some try to make the point that the problem of work-family conflict transcends gender. They are right in some respects but in our view it's also still *about* gender" (p. 11; emphasis in original); "It is time for gender equity in the workplace and at home" (p. 16); and "Change society's gender ideology through education and socialization" (p. 152).

Friedman and Greenhaus could actually serve as poster boys for Schumpeter's process of creative destruction. Their book is compelling proof that there is nothing conservative about capitalism. "Keep the *revolution* going," they argue. "The struggle for the creation of new and more varied lifestyle options is far from over." Existing "hierarchies" must be shattered. These professors of management also insist that Americans "must be prepared to make the most of the *brave new world*" lying in the future, in order to advance "the *workplace revolution*."

What specifically needs to be changed? The authors say that women must be pulled more completely into the corporate world, for "success in *the brave new world* of twenty-first century careers" requires people able to handle ambiguity, manage many simultaneous tasks, and build networks; and "Women seem to be more skilled in these areas than men." The latter, then, need to be weaned from their careers and trained to spend more time in childcare and eldercare. Why? Because in "contrast with mothers . . ., it is *less* career involvement for a father that increases his psychological availability to his children." They suggest that "innovative summer camps" be used to indoctrinate children into the needed revolution: "let's open our children's minds to challenging the traditional gender roles" in these boot camps for the post-family order.

Friedman and Greenhaus praise Hillary Rodham Clinton's book, *It Takes a Village*, for its "powerful message" that "each of us—society as a whole—bears responsibility for all children, even other people's children." To meet this obligation, government subsidies should "significantly increase the quality and affordability of child care for working parents." Family leave measures should be strengthened. And more caregivers should be recruited, trained, and paid with state funds.

Amidst long passages lamenting the unmet potential of "Clinton the listener" (tragically undone by "an out-of-bounds sexual appetite"), Mona Harrington's *Care and Equality: Inventing a New Family Politics* offers roughly the same argument.[5] Following the movement of most women into work outside the home, "the country's care system [is] collapsing." The need now is to "explicitly link economics and the function of caregiving" and build a new public system of care. This initiative "must begin with a clear view of the *unfair* allocation to women of the major costs of care giving." Instead, a "new family order" must be created, where men take on more care duties while women focus on career development. The author praises former president Bill Clinton's use of the term "Corporate Citizen" for underscoring that corporations are, indeed, citizens of the modern polity, with their own set of responsibilities for creating this new family order.

Harrington urges no less than a political revolution, where "care" is added to the existing pantheon of national social values: "liberty, equality, and justice." In practice, she says, the joint goals of "care" and "equality" can only be achieved through a vast expansion of the welfare state. The author's agenda includes extending the existing Family and Medical Leave Act to cover *all* employees and to supply paid leave (just as in "Sweden"). "Joint corporate-governmental contributions" should be used to create "a guaranteed annual income" for all households. "For children, *the familiar list* includes support for high-quality paid day care and tax credits for families using it, support for early childhood care and education, and strong support for after-school programs." Government-corporate subsidies should provide thorough training and higher salaries for caregivers. There should also be "greatly increased governmental funding" for community centers offering elder care. Harrington's "new politics of social responsibility" boils down to this: the home largely disappears as a functional place; employers gain *all* the productive adults; governments claim the children, the old, and the sick.

Theda Skocpol is a more serious scholar and more judicious in her analysis and conclusions. Her earlier book, *Protecting Soldiers and Mothers: The Political Origins of Social Policy in the United States*, was a reasonably accurate history of the "maternalism" that guided the earliest federal programs touching on the family. Her turn-of-the-millenium volume, *The Missing Middle: Working Families and the Future of American Social Policy*, has a similar depth.[6] She is aware, for example, of the "self-interest" held by corporations in the weakening of family bonds. Skocpol honestly reports how changes in family structure—particularly the rise of single-parent households through out-of-wedlock births and divorce—have been a major cause of mounting poverty. She pinpoints the social devaluation of marriage and parenthood and honestly acknowledges that the passing of the "family wage" regime came at some considerable social cost. And her book includes a sensible discussion of tax policy and families.

But in the end, she throws her argument into the hands of state capitalism and its Siamese twin, the complete welfare state. As Skocpol explains, "it is a myth that vibrant market capitalism and adequate social supports for working families cannot go hand in hand." While acknowledging that the existing Social Security system greatly benefits the elderly at the expense of young workers, she recoils from talk of cutting back. The "best response," she reasons, "may be to increase the stake of people of all ages—and generations—in national social programs." Her "inclusive and redistributive social security system" would include universal health insurance and paid family leaves. It would require "repeated increases in the minimum wage" and "a national system of subsidized child care," with state support given to both institutions and families.

As with all the authors described above, she ultimately sees the issue boiling down to the quiet burial of the homemaker and fulltime mother: "at the turn of the twenty-first century, participation in the wage-employment system is universally understood as desirable for all adults, men and women, mothers and fathers alike." Home production and the home economy must give way to reliance on the wage and the state. Using classic Democratic Socialist language, Skocpol concludes that "it will be necessary to revalue national government as an instrument for addressing broadly shared needs in the name of democratically shared values." Or put another way, for "work and family . . . to mesh more smoothly," families must submit to the corporate state.

Fortunately, there are two other books offering alternate interpretations of the "work-family crisis." Given its title, *Love & Economics: Why the Laissez-Faire Family Doesn't Work*, the reader might expect to find in the first of this pair but another justification for expanding the welfare state.[7] However, the author Jennifer Roback Morse has a very different agenda. A professor of economics for fifteen years at Yale and George Mason Universities, and currently affiliated with California's Hoover Institution, Morse writes as a libertarian who has discovered through painful experience the limits to classical liberal thought.

Her awakening came, it appears, as the consequence of adopting a two-and-a-half-year-old boy from a Romanian orphanage. While her natural-born daughter matured normally, she said that "the developmental path of our son has been circuitous, painful, and slow, unlike anything we could have ever predicted. We had to provide explicit instructions for our son to learn tasks our daughter picked up effortlessly: making eye contact, making the most elementary sounds, playing peek-a-boo, noticing other people, even smiling." Morse learned by experience that babies are not born oriented to the good: "they are just cute savages who have the potential to be civilized. It is not a foregone conclusion that any particular child will be civilized." Morse concluded that the real work of life is not to be found in the domain of paid employment: "The real world is the world around the kitchen table, the world of the nursery, the world of the bedroom." She also learned that the laissez-faire principles of competition, efficiency, and pursuit of self-interest could not be extended into families and other face-to-face communities: they did not "provide the social glue for the good society."

One of her most candid admissions follows from a discussion of "attachment disorder" in children. She describes:

> . . . a child who does not care what anyone thinks of him. The disapproval of others does not deter the child from bad behavior because no other person . . . matters to the child. . . . The child does whatever he thinks he can get away with, no matter the cost to others. He does not monitor his own behavior, so authority figures must constantly be aware of him and watch him. He lies if he thinks it is advantageous to lie . . . He shows no regret at hurting another person . . . [H]e may become a sophisticated manipulator. . . .

Who is this child, Morse asks? "Why, it is *homo economicus*," the rational, calculating, economic man of libertarian theory whose "actions are governed by the self-interested calculations of costs and benefits."

From this perspective, she concludes that something is fundamentally wrong in modern Western society. Without using his name, she acknowledges Schumpeter's dilemma: "Our new problem is that the family bonds that earlier generations of political theorists could take for granted have become so weakened that the very fabric of social life is threatened." And Morse even identifies the essence of the real problem: political dominance by an "ideological cocktail" composed of "left-wing self-esteem feminism and right-wing income maximizing capitalism."

But at this point her argument falters, for she does not acknowledge the remainder of Schumpeter's argument: that capitalism's own nervous energy and value imperialism undoes the inherited institutions that might keep it humane. Instead, Morse implicitly holds to a view of market neutrality: the problem lies with bad people and bad ideas, not within the system itself. Kept in their proper place, markets can work just fine. And so, her proposed antidotes to family decline wind up fairly anemic. Still the libertarian here, Morse would cut back the state by reducing the sway of Social Security, spiking welfare to single mothers, taking moral education out of the public schools, and tempering the power of child-protection agencies. Her long and sometimes poignant passages on the meaning of love and sacrifice also imply a call to mothers to return home voluntarily to care for their children. All

11

of these are reasonable, even good ideas. But they seem to float in the air, only encountering the margins of the aggressive new family order of the corporate statists.

The second volume is made of sterner stuff. Brian Robertson's *There's No Place Like Work: How Business, Government, and Our Obsession With Work Have Driven Parents from Home* rests on fewer illusions, more historical insights, and full recognition of the Schumpter argument: capitalism's marketplace is not neutral ground.[8] The author offers a lengthy and solid history of the "family wage" regime, showing how this mix of cultural pressures and law limited industrial intrusion into the family for about a century. Like Schumpeter, he sees the falling marital birth rate as a sign of family decay. He also gives specific examples of a feminist-driven capitalism's creative destruction of the home:

- "The transformation of the father-ideal from chief breadwinner to chief consumer was probably already accomplished before the transformation of the mother from homemaker to working mom."
- "The feminist solution . . . has also succeeded, in many homes, in making domestic work just one more commodity for which the market has a price tag."
- "[W]hat began to happen in the 1960s was a large-scale cultural capitulation to the feminist romanticization of the marketplace . . . as well as an increasing demand on the part of business for female labor."

Indeed, Robertson ably identifies some of the key steps in rearing the new corporate state on the bones of the autonomous family. In 1957, for example, the US Department of Labor and business groups jointly held a conference on "Work in the Lives of Married Women." At the very height of the postwar baby boom and the evident surge in female domesticity, corporate and government economists agreed that only the labor of married women and mothers could overcome looming "manpower" shortages. Some years later *The Economist* magazine, with its characteristic blunt honesty, made more explicit what business had to gain: "[w]omen are proving a godsend to many [American] employers. They usually cost less to employ than men, are more prepared to be flexible and less inclined to pick up a fuss if working conditions are poor. . . . Employers like them because they . . . command lower pay, and because part-timers can be pushed harder while they are at work."

Robertson also describes recent episodes of rational cost accounting at work in the post-family order. One employer gives a 25 percent pay raise to new mothers if they return more quickly to their corporate tasks.

A life insurance company has found "lactation support rooms" to be an efficient tool, saving $1,435 and three days of sick leave per breastfed baby: "a three to one return on their investment." Such developments remind Robertson of Hilaire Belloc's prediction, early in the twentieth century, that the threat to the West's freedom did not arise from socialism per se, "but from an unholy alliance of big government and big business" where workers would find security in "government regulation, confirming the economic dominance of larger corporations."

The author faults an American conservatism which exalts the unfettered market as its first principle. He also offers a very different policy agenda. Massive tax relief tied to marriage and the number of children might serve as a workable substitute for the "family wage." And the protection and encouragement of home schooling could be a promising way to start bringing real functions back into the home circle.

Also at the turn of the millennium, word came from Asia of a remarkable change: the Communist Party of China would open its membership to capitalists. Most Western observers saw this as still another symbolic triumph by the free market system over its arch-collectivist foe. But another interpretation is possible. Perhaps this is a symbol of a different victory, the triumph of a global capitalism in league with welfare socialism to advance the true revolution built through creative destruction. Seen this way, "Capitalists in the Communist Party" represent no advance of liberty, but rather the deepened slavery of atomized individuals, now dependent jointly on the megacorporations for normal sustenance and on the mother state for security and "care." This is, I believe, how the British Distributists of the 1920s, the American Agrarians of the 1930s, and an Austrian American economist named Schumpeter of the 1940s would have viewed the capitalist-Communist hybrid.

Notes

1. Joseph A. Schumpeter, *Capitalism, Socialism, and Democracy* (New York: Harper and Brothers, 1942).
2. See: Alva Myrdal, *Nation and Family* (London: Kegan Paul, Trench, Trubner & Co., 1942).
3. Jody Heymann, *The Widening Gap: Why America's Working Families are in Jeopardy and What Can Be Done About It* (New York: Basic Books, 2000).
4. Stewart D. Friedman and Jeffrey H. Greenhaus, *Work and Family: Allies or Enemies? What Happens When Business Professionals Confront Life Choices* (New York: Oxford University Press, 2000).

5. Mona Harrington, *Care and Equality: Inventing a New Family Politics* (New York: Alfred A. Knopf, 1999).

6. Theda Skocpol, *The Missing Middle: Working Families and the Future of American Social Policy* (New York: W.W. Norton & Company, 2000).

7. Jennifer Roback Morse, *Love & Economics: Why the Laissez-Faire Family Doesn't Work* (Dallas: Spence Publishing Co., 2001).

8. Brian C. Robertson, *There's No Place Like Work: How Business, Government, and Our Obsession with Work Have Driven Parents from Home* (Dallas: Spence Publishing Co., 2000).

2

The Curious Case of
Gender Equality

A decade ago, I was sitting before a fire in the delightful, wood-paneled, common room of the Tabard Inn, an old hotel near DuPont Circle in Washington, DC. I was with a group of historians, some of whom could be fairly labeled the leaders in their specialties; two had won Pulitzer Prizes. It was evening and the conviviality was encouraged by the fruit of the vine and the distiller's art. This group, I underscore, was exclusively male.

At one point, the conversation turned to the question: Over the course of the twentieth century, which ideology had enjoyed the greatest success? What world-view had been most influential in reshaping ideas, attitudes, and institutions? We considered the last flowering and then the ruin of monarchism in the fires of World War I, the rise and eventual defeat of Fascism, Nazism, and Japanese Imperialism, the Bolshevik victory in Russia and the spread of Communism to Eastern Europe, China, Southeast Asia, Africa, and Latin America, the development of Democratic Socialism in Scandinavia and its spread in Europe after World War II, the rise of new nationalisms such as Zionism and Pan-Arabism, the spread of Democratic Liberalism aided and abetted by the success of American arms, the re-emergence of a militant Islam in the latter decades of the century, and so on. But in the end, we concluded that the greatest success had been registered by a surprise candidate: the ideology known as liberal or equity feminism.

Now, I am not sure whether this conclusion would have survived a fresh, more sober conversation in the light of the next morning. Perhaps the academics in the group were simply discouraged by recent faculty meetings. All the same, I do want to explore here the nature and consequence of the ideology of strict gender equality which has enjoyed, by any measure, at least remarkable success during the last forty years.

An intriguing academic journal sprang into existence fifteen years ago. Called *Feminist Economics*, it underscores the comprehensive sweep of the feminist world-view. Like any other ideology worth its salt, feminism has its own theology, its own psychology, its own science, its own history, its own anthropology, and even its own economics, with special journals of academic inquiry created in each discipline. The attraction of *Feminist Economics* lies partly in the unexpected, but entertaining articles that appear. Take, for example, the essay "Towards Lesbian, Gay, and Bisexual Perspectives in Economics." It notes, by way of explanation, that "Lesbians—females who live by rejecting that primary form of obligation, obligation to men—bring about lesbian economics," one reflecting debates over "liberal, radical, or socialist/Marxist changes and on the pluses and minuses of poststructuralist queer theory."[1] You will not find that kind of analysis in, say, *The Wall Street Journal*.

Feminist Economics also carries narrative reports on feminist success in restructuring American life. For example, an article by Harriet Presser of the University of Maryland's Center on Population, Gender, and Social Inequality describes the effort by "a small group of feminist social scientists" in the late 1970s to force the US Census Bureau to stop using the term, "head of household." Under this pressure, the Census Bureau did drop the term in the 1980 count, replacing it with the label, "householder." Dr. Presser complains, though, that the term "head of household" has somehow survived in the Bureau's General Social Survey, and notes:

> The reluctance of the research community to drop the concept of "head" reveals how ingrained the ideological notion of an authority structure within the family is.[2]

Indeed, another fascinating aspect of the journal are those articles—not infrequent—where feminist theorists confront the distortions of human life and human nature mandated by their own ideology. For instance, in the article "Subsidizing Child Care by Mothers at Home," Barbara Bergmann of American University argues against the idea of extending tax credits for early child care—currently available only if children are put into paid day care—to parents who care for their children at home. She acknowledges that such an extension of the credit would expand child care choices for all women and would be very popular. But she continues: "The ability and willingness of mothers of very young children to work at jobs has been central to the changes in women's status. . . . All women workers have better job opportunities when the custom is for most new mothers to return to work very soon after the birth of a child." Bergmann underscores that "the provision of significantly large benefits to mothers caring for their own children . . . puts social pressure on all mothers to stay home." She reasons: "Anything that increases the social pressure for having children cared for full time by their own mothers is a step back toward rigid gender roles, with each gender limited to sex-appropriate activities."[3] In short, the feminist project requires that women be separated from their babies at the earliest feasible time and that women have only one practical way of reconciling work and family: the day care center.

More telling is an insightful article by Judith Galtry of Australia's Victoria University of Wellington: "Suckling and Silence in the USA: The Costs and Benefits of Breastfeeding." The author notes the overwhelming evidence of the benefits provided to women, children, and society by breastfeeding. Women who have breastfed report significantly lower rates of breast cancer and ovarian cancer and less osteoporosis in later life. Children who were breastfed as infants are also much healthier than bottle-fed babies. In industrialized nations, breastfed children have in general a lower mortality rate and are far less likely to face sudden infant death syndrome. Breastfed babies record significantly lower rates of pneumonia, bacteremia, meningitis, serious ear infections, gastrointestinal and lower respiratory tract disease, and a number of chronic diseases later in life. Breastfeeding also enhances the growth and development of the brain and central nervous system of *both* preterm and full-term babies. Society also benefits. Breastfed children do better in school and accrue much lower medical costs. Even employers gain, for the absenteeism rate of working mothers is seven times lower among breastfeeding mothers when compared to the mothers of babies fed on infant formula.

And yet, Professor Galtry notes, feminist theorists retain at best a stony "silence" and at worst an outright *hostility* toward breastfeeding. Even the argument that slightly over half of the industrialized world's infants will grow up to be *women* leaves the equity feminist unmoved.

Why? For the clear reason that breastfeeding—even more than pregnancy and childbirth—exposes the fatal flaw in equity feminist theory: women *are* different from men, with effects on their lives and on the lives of others and of whole societies that cannot be ignored. Insistence on "equal treatment" between men and women in parenting creates what the author calls "an obvious, but generally unarticulated, dilemma." She also notes another curious fact: the highest rates of breastfeeding in the US and Britain are found among wealthy, white, professional women. They are the ones who are able to take advantage of parental leave policies, without fear of impoverishment; and it is *their* children who gain an advantage in *their* life prospects.

Equity feminists worry that acknowledging the benefits of breastfeeding might "undermine gender-neutral leave provisions," or "reinforce the notion that childrearing and other household chores are primarily the responsibility of women," or encourage "another version of pay for housewives," or—most perversely—create the perception that women are "in need of paternalistic protection" and so define women "in terms of their presumed or actual maternal role." Phrased another way, equity feminists see more cancer and death among women, higher infant mortality, diminished health and intellectual prospects for all children, and heightened racial and social class differences as acceptable prices to pay to avoid such "maternal" ends.[4]

The core equity feminist dilemma, of course, is that this movement—like all modern ideological movements—is at war with human nature. The equity feminist wants to deny the realities of sex-difference and engineer a new human type: the androgynous being. In practice, though, the attempt is no less amazing and no less futile than the effort by the German Nazis to create The New Aryan Man or the effort by the Bolsheviks to create The New Soviet Man.

For the natural sciences reveal, over and again, the impossibility of the androgyny project. In the fields of human biology and biochemistry, for example, dramatic findings highlight the important effects of hormonal and psychological differences between women and men: in everything from the functioning of the nervous system and the brain to emotional drives. These lessons, of course, do not teach that one sex is "better" than or "superior" to the other; such claims are at once wrong and irrelevant. The true lesson is the *remarkable* complementarity of woman and man: in the creation of families and in the rearing of children, men and women are designed to work together, each bringing special gifts and aptitudes which make the union greater or stronger than the sum of its parts.

This is why research shows:

- That *children* raised outside intact, two-natural-parent families are *forty* times *more* likely to be physically or sexually abused than are children raised within intact families.[5]

- Or that "maternal care" of young children provides "a protective factor" in psychological well-being that neither fathers nor non-parental caregivers can provide.[6]
- Or that the level of the male hormone, testosterone, goes down among married men, who by marrying become *less aggressive* and *more cooperative* in socially constructive ways: that is, they became *gentle men.*[7]

Indeed, even the theorists of evolution testify to family living as a defining trait of humanity. In his seminal article for *Science* magazine, paleo-anthropologist C. Owen Lovejoy marshalls the evidence showing that both human survival as a species and evolutionary progress have depended on what he calls "the unique sexual reproductive behavior" of humankind. Lovejoy shows that the human family system, rooted in complementary pair-bonding, reaches back hundreds of thousands of years; he even implies that the very definition of "human" rests on this family behavior. As Lovejoy writes:

> [B]oth advanced material culture and the Pleistocene accelera-
> tion in brain development are *sequelae* to an already established
> hominid character system, which included *intensified parenting and
> social relationships, monogamous pair-bonding, specialized sexual-
> reproductive behavior* [by male and female], and bipedality. It implies
> that the *nuclear family* and human sexual behavior may have their
> ultimate origin long before the dawn of the Pleistocene.[8]

That is, even before the paleo-anthropologists' early man began to walk on two legs, he was already living in a recognizably human family system built on the complementarity and cooperation of the sexes.

Indeed, there is growing evidence pointing to the looming failure of the feminist experiment. A recent article in *Social Forces* examines seven surveys between 1974 and 1997 of attitudes toward masculinity and femininity. Unexpectedly, the researchers report that "the major findings have been stability [or] increasing sex typing. Of the twenty-four comparisons [between men and women investigated in this study], ten have shown stability and eleven an increase in sex typing, the strongest of these being the increased femininity of females, both in the ratings of the typical female by both males and females and in the self-ratings of the female respondents." Noting the failure of feminist sociological theory to account for this, the researchers conclude that this strengthening of gender stereotypes reflects "predispositions based on *innate* patterns as posited by the evolutionary model."[9]

But if this is true—if gender stereotyping that defies feminist theory is growing stronger—why does our current national situation seem so completely different, even disordered?

The new problem is that key American political and economic institutions have been distorted over the last forty years, during the period of equity feminism's institutional dominance. To explain how that occurred, I need to say more about the history of equity feminism in twentieth century America.

A casual look at America today shows pro-life and pro-family voters largely attached to the Republican Party and so in political alliance with Big Business. Equity feminism, meanwhile, dominates in the Democratic Party, in alliance with the labor unions and the pro-abortion cause. These are, however, historically unusual coalitions.

Indeed, from the 1920s until the early 1960s, the Republican Party was *the* party of equity feminism, a movement which had a natural bond with the interests of big business: *both* were products of the liberal vision focused on the priority of the individual; and *both* wanted women in the fulltime workforce. When the National Woman's Party crafted the proposed "Equal Rights Amendment" (ERA) to the US Constitution back in 1923, it was Republicans who first introduced the measure in the US House and Senate. The National Association of Manufacturers, seeking access to cheap female labor, was the first major national organization to endorse the ERA. Indeed, there is some evidence that the Manufacturers Association covertly funded the radical National Woman's Party during the 1920s and 1930s.[10] The Republican Party was the first party to include the ERA in its national platform. And, after the Birth Control Federation of America cleverly changed its name to Planned Parenthood, this organization became a favorite charity among Republican Women's Clubs.

The Democrats, meanwhile, were the party more-or-less defending small property, Christian sexual morality, and traditional family values. So-called "social feminists" or "maternalists" in the Party such as Frances Perkins and Molly Dewson gave first priority to the protection of motherhood and traditional homes. They believed in equality for women and men in civic and legal rights, but also in the political recognition of differences between the sexes in function. Central to "maternalist" economic thinking was support for The Family Wage regime, a system of custom and law that delivered to a father and husband a wage sufficient to support a mother and children at home;

and a system that celebrated and protected the roles of homemaker and mother. As Julia Lathrop, Chief of the US Children's Bureau during the Woodrow Wilson years, explained:

> The power to maintain a decent family living standard is the primary essential of child welfare. This means a living wage and wholesome working life for the man, a good and skillful mother at home to keep the house and comfort all within it. Society can afford *no less* and can afford *no exceptions*. This is a universal need.[11]

As implied here, the primary support for the "family wage" came to be a system of "job segregation by gender": the cultural assumption that there were "men's jobs" and "women's jobs," and that men's jobs deserved higher compensation because they commonly supported a wife and children, as well as the man. This method of taming capitalism's Creative Destruction actually proved to be highly effective, helping to produce *both* economic prosperity *and* the Marriage and Baby Booms of the 1940s and 1950s.

Compared to today, though, this world that I just described almost seems to be an alternate moral universe. How did we get from there to here?

Actually, we can trace the change to a single day, *February 8, 1964*, when the American social-political order underwent a seismic shift, and equity-feminism won arguably its most important policy victory. But it is a change that you will never read about in a civics or history textbook, because it is also—for feminists—a tale of embarrassing political farce, one exhibiting the dangerous and destructive force of the concept of equality, once loosened.

The occasion was debate in the US House of Representatives over the proposed Civil Rights Act of 1964. The language of the bill on that Saturday morning—as first drafted at the Lyndon Johnson White House—aimed at ending discrimination "on the basis of race, color, religion, or national origin" in the areas of voting, public accommodations and education, federally assisted programs, and private employment. Reading between the lines, it was clear that the latter provision on private employment—Title VII—would renew an old maternalist goal from the New Deal years: to remove those job barriers resting on race prejudice that prevented African American men from being good fathers, husbands, and breadwinners. Advocates used an argument that would surface again in the famed Moynihan Report a year later: if the traditional family home *was* the basis of American civilization, then full citizenship for black Americans required shoring up the economic side of their faltering family system. Disproportionately characterized by matriarchy, female-headed households, and illegitimacy, "the Negro-American family"—as it was then called—needed to be reconfigured on the prevailing breadwinner/homemaker model found among whites. If this could be done, racial equality would result.[12]

Yet Southern Democrats in the House chamber, their backs to the wall, had resolved on a desperate strategy. Some, we may infer, were defending the segregated order; all presumably opposed this proposed extension of federal power into private life. Seeking a "killer" amendment to the Civil Rights bill, these "Dixiecrats" urged a change in the language of Title VII that would—they thought—expose the danger of the concept of "equality." Congressman Howard Smith of Virginia rose on that February day and, with a broad smile, proposed that the word "sex" be added to the list of prohibited discriminations in employment under Title VII.[13] To the laughter of his colleagues, he reported on a letter he had received from a woman protesting the excess number of American females, when compared to the count of American men, revealed by the 1960 Census. Smith read:

> Just why the Creator would set up such an imbalance of spinsters, shutting off the "right" of every female to have a husband of her own is, of course, known only to nature. But I am sure you will agree that this is a grave injustice to womankind and something the Congress and President Johnson should take immediate steps to correct.

After making his little joke, though, Smith moved to other, real issues: "Now, I am very serious about this amendment," he told his colleagues. "I think we all recognize . . . that all throughout industry women are discriminated against in that . . . they do not get as high compensation for their work as do the majority [sic] sex."

As the debate took form, Smith's Dixiecrat colleagues added their sometimes whimsical support. J. Russell Tuten of Georgia said that as "a man, which places me in the minority and makes me a second class citizen—and the fact that I am white and from the South—I look forward to claiming my rights under this legislation." Joe Pool of Texas argued that the amendment would "safeguard American women from such inequities with regard to their civil rights as are now threatened in the pending civil rights bill." And L. Mendel Rivers of South Carolina praised the proposed change for "making it possible for the white

Christian woman to receive the same consideration for employment as the colored woman."

In retrospect, it is clear that a half century of political reforms aimed at restoring "the traditional family" and built on the family-wage ideal hung in the balance. And it appears that the heirs of this maternalist or social feminist vision, and of the New Deal policies that had solidly embedded it into the law, understood that their legacy was threatened. Pro-family Democrats mounted their last stand.

Emanuel Celler, Democrat from New York, chairman of the House Judiciary Committee, floor leader for the Civil Rights bill, and a Jew, rose to challenge Smith. Notably, Congressman Celler argued for the natural inequality of woman and man:

> You know, the French have a phrase for it when they speak of women and men . . . "vive la différence." I think the French are right.
>
> Imagine the upheaval that would result from the adoption of blanket language requiring total [sexual] equality. Would male citizens be justified in insisting that women share with them the burdens of compulsory military service? What would become of traditional family relationships? What about alimony? . . . Would fathers rank equally with mothers in the right of custody to children? . . . This is the entering wedge, an amendment of this sort.

Representative Celler also noted that the Women's Bureau of the US Department of Labor (long a maternalist stronghold) opposed this amendment, because sex discrimination involved "problems significantly different" from race and other factors covered by the bill's language.

Edith Green, a Democratic Congresswoman from Oregon, attacked Smith's amendment as an attempt to "jeopardize" the primary purpose of the Civil Rights Act: "For every discrimination that has been made against a woman in this country there has been ten times as much discrimination against the Negro. . . . Whether we want to admit it or not, the main purpose of this legislation today is to try to end the discrimination . . . against Negroes." Moreover, she insisted that there were real "biological differences" between men and women that must be taken into account "in regard to employment."

But the equity feminists found on the Republican side of Congress, having spent forty years in the political wilderness, sensed on that day their extraordinary, if peculiar, opportunity. Congresswoman Katharine St. George, a Republican from New York, took the podium and suggested that foes of the "sex" amendment still saw women as "chattels." She added: "Why should women be denied equality of opportunity? Why should women be denied equal pay for equal work?" Congresswoman Catherine May, a Republican from Washington, cited the deep concerns of the National Woman's Party over the effect of an unamended Title VII on "the white, native-born American woman of Christian religion."

Much to Smith's surprise, this unexpected coalition of Republican equity feminists and Dixiecrat segregationists carried the day, on a vote of 168 to 133. Two days later, the House approved the Civil Rights Act, as amended. The measure went on to the Senate, where Hubert Humphrey pushed the measure through unchanged, throttling a Southern filibuster.

So, in July, the Civil Rights Act of 1964, as amended, became law. A measure originally designed to aid black men—five percent of the population—was redirected to give aid to white women—45 percent of the population. The new Equal Employment Opportunities Commission, according to one friendly analyst, soon "converted Title VII into a magna carta for female workers, grafting to it a set of rules and regulations that certainly could *not* have passed Congress in 1964, and perhaps not a decade later, either."[14]

Most significantly, the Commission quickly eliminated sex-specific hiring, seniority, and promotion practices. Again, it was these forms of job segregation by gender that had long served as the buttresses to America's family wage system, guiding men toward the higher-paid positions and women toward the lower ones or toward home. But now the economic foundation of households would shift. The flow of married women into the labor force accelerated. In consequence, it became more difficult to sustain the "traditional American family"—white and black—on one income. As female wages rose, male breadwinners working full-time experienced a 28 percent decline in real wages over the next two decades.

In the early 1970s, women such as Phyllis Schlafly would battle Republican hierarchies to end that party's support for the ERA and liberalized abortion: by 1980 so-called "Reagan Democrats"—notably working class Catholics and Southern evangelicals—moved into the Republican camp. Equity feminists migrated the other way, producing the anomalous political situation in which we live today. Beyond party politics, though, we can see here how the feminist values of radical individualism and strict gender equality undermined arrangements that had sustained families within the dynamic turbulence of the modern economic order.

What, then, might the future hold? I am confident of one thing: Feminist leaders are right to be worried. Their institutional and policy ascendance will be undone, for it violates the deeper truths of human nature that will win out in the end.

Relative to the "family wage" ideal just explored, it may be that incremental tax policies will restore significant protection to married-couple families and their children. For example, the indexing to inflation of the child exemption in the federal income tax in 1986, the creation of the child-tax-credit in 1996, and repairs to the "marriage penalty" in the income tax have already begun to restore some economic protections to marriage and childbearing. Of more direct threat to the equity feminist agenda, members of Congress have recently introduced bills to extend the child care tax credit to *stay-at-home parents* (the very idea denounced by Barbara Bergmann in *Feminist Economics*).

But it may also be that "equity feminism" will be undone by the feminists themselves. The "social feminist" or "maternalist" vision focused on "equality in rights, difference in function." After its own intellectual exile for the last fifty years, *maternalism* may now be coming back. Another article—again in *Feminist Economics*—brilliantly lays out the case for maternalism. Entitled "The Other Economy," the essay argues that the most important questions that feminist economists should ask "are related to caring and children."[15] Author Susan Donath argues that mainstream economics, with its focus on competitive production and exchange, is *too simple* a theory to account for women's caring work. Children, too, "tumble out of every category economists try to put them in."[16] There are two economies, she concludes: one focused on markets and competition where money is the medium of exchanges; and the "other economy" focused on gifts, reciprocity, and caring where love is the medium of exchange. "In my view," Monath concludes, "the feminist economics project is concerned with describing and analyzing the *other* economy, both in its own right, and as it interacts with the market economy."

The author makes other important points. In services such as early child care and elder care, she notes, "few or no productivity gains are possible," meaning that purchased day care and institutional nursing care can rarely—if ever—be cost effective, once quality of care is taken into account. The exception to this comes only when the wealthy employ the very poorest or illegal immigrants to provide child care or elder care, revealing again the degree to which day care rests on the distortion or exploitation of the lives of the poor. To underscore the point, she notes that a 1995 plan put forward by equity feminists—called "Help for Working Parents"—would provide a working mother with $9,500 in annual child care subsidy; while mothers employed full-time at a minimum wage job could earn only $8,500: this would amount to a net *loss* to the market economy of at least $1,000, not to mention the negative psychological and medical costs of group care on children.[17]

Donath so confirms what the English journalist G.K. Chesterton first reported eighty years before: "The whole [day care argument] really rests on a plutocratic illusion of an infinite supply of servants. . . . Ultimately, we are arguing that a woman should not be a mother to her own baby, but a mother to somebody else's. But it will not work. Not even on paper. We cannot all live by taking in each other's washing, especially in the form of pinafores."[18]

In short, through this article we see the journal *Feminist Economics* arriving at the same conclusions regarding child care and economic justice for families, as did the great Catholic Agrarian, Chesterton. Perhaps the heavens have parted as well; or perhaps hell has just frozen over. More likely, the innate truths regarding the natural family have found expression in an unlikely place.

Notes

1. M.V. Lee Badgett and Prue Hyman, "Introduction: Towards Lesbian, Gay, and Bisexual Perspectives in Economics: Why and How They Make a Difference," *Feminist Economics* 4 (1998): 50.
2. Harriet B. Presser, "Decapitating the U.S. Census Bureau's 'Head of Household': Feminist Mobilization in the 1970's," *Feminist Economics* 4 (1998): 145–58.
3. Barbara R. Bergmann, "Subsidizing Child Care by Mothers at Home," *Feminist Economics* 6 (2000): 77–78.
4. Judith Galtry, "Suckling and Silence in the USA: The Costs and Benefits of Breastfeeding," *Feminist Economics* 3 (1997): 1–24.
5. Joy J. Lightcap, Jeffrey A. Kurland, and Robert L. Burgess, "Child Abuse: A Test of Some Predictions of Evolutionary Theory," *Ethology and Sociobiology* 3 (1982): 61–67.
6. Mohammadreza Hojat, "Satisfaction with Early Relationships with Parents and Psychosocial Attributes in Adulthood: Which Parent Contributes More?" *The Journal of Genetic Psychology* 159 (1998): 202–20.
7. From *Social Forces*.
8. C. Owen Lovejoy, "The Origin of Man," *Science* 211 (January 1981): 348 (emphasis added).

9. Lloyd B. Lueptow, Lori Garovich-Szabo, and Margaret B. Lueptow, "Social Change and the Persistence of Sex Typing 1974–1997," *Social Forces* 80 (2001): 1–35.
10. Reported in: Lillian Holmen Mohr, *Frances Perkins* (n.p.: North River Press, 1979): 192; and Mary Anderson and Mary N. Winslow, *Women at Work: The Autobiography of Mary Anderson* (Minneapolis: University of Minnesota Press, 1951), 171.
11. Quotation from: Molly Ladd-Taylor, *Mother-Work: Women, Child Welfare, and the State, 1890–1930* (Urbana, IL: University of Illinois Press, 1994), 91.
12. See: Lee Rainwater and William L. Yancey, eds., *The Moynihan Report and the Politics of Controversy* (Cambridge, MA: M.I.T. Press, 1969), 39–132.
13. From: *The Congressional Record: Proceedings and Debates of the 88th Congress. Second Session* (Vol. 110, pt. 2), February 8, 1964: 2577–87.
14. Donald Allen Robinson, "Two Movements in Pursuit of Equal Opportunity," *Signs: Journal of Women in Culture and Society* 4, no. 3 (1979): 427.
15. Susan Donath, "The Other Economy: A Suggestion for a Distinctively Feminist Economics," *Feminist Economics* 4 (2000): 115–23.
16. A quotation borrowed by Donath from analyst Nancy Folbre.
17. Donath, "The Other Economy," 121–22.
18. G.K. Chesterton, "The Superstition of Divorce," in *Collected Works, Vol. IV: Family, Society, Politics*, ed. George Marlin (San Francisco: Ignatius Press, 1987), 254.

3

The "Good War": World War II and the Displacement of Community in America

Stubborn American commitments in Iraq and Afghanistan have cast in ever sharper contrast the place of World War II as America's "Good War." What made it good? Beyond our clearly winning, I would highlight three factors.

First, we had easily identifiable and wonderfully evil enemies. The German Nazis were foes of Christianity, murderers of the Jews, racist monsters who killed and looted without restraint, the enemies of Western Civilization or any civilization. By late 1941, the Italian Fascists stood revealed as thuggish, albeit fairly inept opportunists: cowardly bullies. The Japanese militarists who designed the sneak attack on Pearl Harbor swept away all doubts about the future of the Pacific: this brutal Axis ally of German and Italy, these perpetrators of the rape of Nanking and the Bataan Death March, these imperialists with their eyes on all of Asia and Oceania, must be stopped.

Second, the "Good War" was a campaign of motion. The most demoralizing aspect of World War I had been the trenches on the Western front. The machine gun ruled those battlefields. Assaults by either side would consume tens of thousands of young lives to gain a few hundred yards of blood-soaked mud. There were a million French and German casualties in the contest over the fort of Verdun alone. Such a conflict produces few heroes. Rather, the main product is despair. In contrast, World War II featured movement. The armored tank trumped the machine gun on land, and huge battles of advance and retreat took place. In the Pacific campaign, great naval air conflicts and island invasions again involved motion. Fear, hope, and exhilaration were the prevailing emotions, not despair.

Finally, the "Good War" was a vast communitarian event: a message that my late mother-in-law, a loyal Franklin Delano Roosevelt (FDR) Democrat, drilled into me during dozens of conversations. Every American, young or old, military or civilian, man or woman, black, white, Native American, or Asian, was mobilized for the duration (even if for Japanese Americans this meant a new life in a concentration camp). All Americans saw their daily lives deeply affected, through air raid drills, rubber drives, food and gasoline rationing, retooled factories, the draft, deferred dreams, heavy taxes, and absent loved ones.

The classic World War II film features the new infantry platoon going into training, with the hard drinking Irish lad from Chicago, the sensitive Jewish youth from Manhattan, the cracker from Georgia, the naïve farm boy from Iowa, and so on. The essential plot shows how the military experience tore down regional and ethnic loyalties, building instead a common Americanism, which inspired the young soldiers to go out and vanquish their fascist foes.

This is, in fact, an appropriate metaphor for what actually took place in America on a vastly larger scale during these years. Driven by military necessity, geographic mobility in the United States reached an unprecedented level. Between December 1941 and March 1945—less than three and a half years—twleve million men and women entered the armed forces. Another 15.3 million American adults left their county of residence, moving to another location for war-related reasons: together, more than one of every four adults. "Never before in the history of our country," the US Bureau of the Census reported, "has there been so great a shuffling and redistribution of population in so short a time."

The South was the region most affected by this war-induced demographic revolution. As Dartmouth sociologist Francis Merrill wrote in 1948: "The war accelerated the prewar migration of Southerners from the rural areas to rapidly growing industrial areas," with a consequent change in what he called "the extreme cultural isolation which formerly characterized farm life in this region."[1]

Merrill's reference to the "extreme cultural isolation" of the rural South is surely the marker of a Yankee analyst. It is also a clue to the broader transformation of community life wrought by World War II. The mobilization of the entire nation to war, the unparalleled motion and mixing of people, and the triumph of nationalism over regionalism and localism meant that some communities would be displaced, while others would emerge or grow. What forms of community dissolved in the crucible of the Good War?

One could look for answers, as Merrill suggests, to the rural South or perhaps to the fate of white ethnic neighborhoods in northern American cities. My focus, though, will be on something of a compromise locale: examining changes in rural life in the upper Mississippi and Ohio river valleys.

In her valuable book, *The Transformation of Rural Life: Southern Illinois, 1890–1990*, anthropologist Jane Adams analyzes in depth the changes over one hundred years in the economy and community life of Union County, Illinois. As late as 1940, she reports, the agriculture-based economy of this place was intact. Its family farms specialized in fruits and vegetables sent north for sale in Chicago. Small dairy and poultry operations were ubiquitous. The annual collective butchering of hogs remained a community ritual. A few small factories making wooden shipping crates and shoes provided supplements to farm incomes. While strained by the Great Depression, Union County's towns and villages were still vital, active places; the town squares and local shops busy; the schools full of children. Rural Union County homes "retained their multiple functions as workshop, warehouse, mess hall, dormitory, recreation center, infirmary, and funeral parlor for the farm and the people who worked on it, and women's and children's hard work was approvingly contrasted with urban idleness."[2]

The contemporary agrarian writer Wendell Berry reports a similar story for the Ohio river valley. During the 1930s, "[t]he economies of many households were [still] small and thorough." These Americans "practiced household husbandry," tended gardens, "fattened meat hogs, milked cows," kept flocks of chickens, used horses or mules for field work, and employed "little children" in their labors. These enterprises "comprised the direct bond between farm and household."[3] Similarly, the villages of northern Kentucky remained whole and complete: "the commercial places in town were still . . . doing business. The people of the town still belonged to it economically."[4]

This apparent rural stability in the prewar Mississippi and Ohio river valleys was reflected in census bureau numbers. In 1900, the total US farm population had reached 29.9 million persons; in 1917, it had reached 32.5 million persons. By 1940, the number on farms still remained just shy of that record figure. Another thirty million persons were in small towns and villages, servicing the farms. Horse power remained competitive with internal combustion power. While the number of tractors had grown from 1,000 in 1910 to 1.4 million in 1940, the number of draught horses still active on farms in that latter year was ten million.

In the agriculture-dominated state of Iowa, a special 1935 census showed that the number of farms reached a record 222,000, with an average size of 155 acres. The state's villages were whole and alive, as well. Rural enthusiast Johnson Brigham aptly labeled Iowa "a commonwealth of small towns," one that "is rising superior to all obstacles and fast-fulfilling its destiny."

The culture of rural America remained vital. In his important book, *Kinship with the Land*, historian E. Bradford Burns recounts the flowering of regionalist thought, writing, and art in Iowa between 1894 and 1942. As late as that end year: "Most of the population worked the land; in one way or another the others depended on it. Rich black soil cut as many furrows into the rural inhabitants as they did into it. Land—close, abundant, productive, all embracing—set not only the economic contours of Iowa but the social and cultural [contours] as well."[5] As Grant Wood, painter of the iconic *American Gothic*, explained: "I'm just a middle western man with a Quaker family background who loves Iowa. . . . At heart I'm a farmer. Pretty darn good farmer, too. Things grow for me. I'm pretty strongly rooted and I like to be home." His 1931–32 art colony in the tiny village of Stone City embodied the American regional artistic revival. Writing in her 1942 novel *New Hope*, the celebrated Iowa author Ruth Suckow described the folk culture of the iconic Iowa village: "All were fellow citizens, all had their share in helping to build up the town. . . . Everywhere could be felt the sense of natural comradeship, of being all together at the start and working together for the future."[6]

The great churning of World War II administered the death stroke, the coup d' grace, to this still complete, if fragile world. Young adults poured off the land: the men to war and the women to urban offices and factories. Adams reports that by January 1944, 1,357 Union County men—over half of their age cohort—were in the military. Labor shortages hit farms hard: "Ask everyone to help with [the] peach crop: shortage of labor is worry to country growers," read one local newspaper headline. In response, real horsepower finally gave way to a surge in tractors. Nationwide, their number rose nearly fourfold during the 1940s. A myriad of federal government agencies also moved into the countryside. Anticipated by the New Deal, this change became a torrent after 1941. "Without people being fully aware of it," writes Adams, "the [Union County] economy shifted from dependence on agriculture and [light] manufacturing to a heavy reliance on government services." As war factories and government bureaucracies transformed rural women into wage workers, the once creative home economy changed as well. As Adams explains, "they no longer had the time to raise a garden and put up quantities of food." Industrial food processors in distant places supplanted them. Adams continues: "At the same time that the informal networks of rural life were becoming frayed, one of the pillars of rural communities, the rural school, was *displaced*" as well. Demanding "modern" education, Illinois officials launched school consolidation drives, changing state school aid formulae so that small rural districts would no longer receive support. The very hearts of small towns—their schools—disappeared.[7]

In more literary fashion, Berry describes the same results: the end of the multitude of villages and small communities, the death of a distinctive agrarian civilization. With the coming of war, he writes, country "[p]eople . . . began to move to the cities, and the machines moved from the cities into the fields."[8] The "good farm economy" weakened and withered. The "wayward" passing of farm land across the generations began. After 1945, Berry reports, the "picture puzzle" that had been his ancestral home became less complete, "the lost pieces were not replaced."[9] Also disappearing were the tasks that only *true* communities could provide: "The care of the old, the care and education of children, family life, neighborly work, the handing down of memory, the care of the earth, respect for nature and wild creatures." The government took over the care of the old and the education of children. The other tasks were mostly forgotten.[10] Within a few decades, the farmland itself was in decline:

> . . . fields and whole farms abandoned, given up with their scars unmended; washing away under the weeds and bushes; fine land put to row crops year after year, without rest or rotation; buildings and fences going down; good houses standing empty, unpainted, their windows broken.[11]

Census bureau numbers reinforce this tale of rapid rural decline. The US farm population fell from 30.5 million in 1940 to twenty-three million by 1950 and only 7.5 million by 1970. Rural children disappeared at an even more rapid pace, turning most remaining farms into working old-folks homes.

Burns underscores how the war accelerated the industrialization of Iowa. In 1939, Iowa had only 65,000 factory workers; by 1947, the number had nearly doubled. More importantly:

> Machinery, the product of progress, [now] separated farmers from the earth they worked. The long period in which farmers actually touched the soil, planted their feet in it, became one with it, ended, a momentous psychological change. The intervention of machinery weakened the sacred relationship between folk and nature.[12]

In February 1942, Grant Wood—the great apostle of Iowa rural regionalism—died of cancer. Ruth Suckow also published her last Iowa-centered novel that year. Other Iowa writers, poets, and artists scattered. As Burns summarizes:

> In the years after 1942, internationalism, standards and life-styles prescribed elsewhere, and goals set by outsiders increasingly triumphed within Iowa. Like most regions of the United States, . . . Iowa was swept into a cultural homogeneity that on most levels denied the individuality of its own past and ignored those lively, perceptive local voices that once called for introspection and valorization of the local.

In words that sum up the war experience for the whole of America, he continued: "Iowans lifted their sights to global horizons, and they, thus far, have found it difficult to focus internally again."[13]

This was the way of life, these were the communities, such were the cultural possibilities, that the "Good War" crushed. Some, of a deterministic bent, would argue that this agrarian America, reaching deep into the nation's past, was doomed in any case. If so, the Good War sharply accelerated the process. My broad argument is that World War II marked a great divide in American social history, where the nation severed its primordial, normative bonds to the agrarian and village ways of life.

Notes

1. Francis E. Merrill, *Social Problems on the Home Front: A Study of War-Time Influences* (New York: Harper and Brothers, 1948), 16–17.
2. Jane Adams, *The Transformation of Rural Life: Southern Illinois, 1890–1990* (Chapel Hill and London: University of North Carolina Press, 1994), 187.
3. Wendell Berry, *The Gift of Good Land* (New York: North Point Press, 1981), 98–99.
4. Wendell Berry, *Jayber Crow* (Washington, DC: Counterpoint, 2000), 4.

5. E. Bradford Burns, *Kinship with the Land: Regionalist Thought in Iowa, 1894–1942* (Iowa City: University of Iowa Press, 1996), 10.
6. Quotations in Burns, *Kinship with the Land*, 149, 170.
7. Adams, *The Transformation of Rural Life*, 157, 160, 198, 214, 217.
8. Wendell Berry, *The Unsettling of America: Culture and Agriculture* (New York: Avon, 1977), 108.
9. Wendell Berry, *Hannah Coulter* (Washington, DC: Shoemaker Hoard, 2004), 38.
10. Wendell Berry, *Sex, Economy, Freedom and Community* (New York: Pantheon, 1992/1993), 133.
11. Berry, *The Unsettling of America*, 108.
12. Burns, *Kinship with the Land*, 166–67.
13. Ibid., 11, 163.

Dissents
(Poetic and Numeric)

4

Hilaire Belloc's Servile State

We recently marked the centennial of English journalist Hilaire Belloc's peculiar book, *The Servile State*. Recent commentators have been unsure where to place this 1912 volume on the ideological spectrum. In the Liberty Fund edition, Robert Nisbet labels Belloc a "libertarian Catholic," a writer taking his inspiration from the nineteenth century's Cardinal Newman and Lord Acton.[1]

In his biography of Belloc, Joseph Pearce also terms his subject's creed "essentially libertarian."[2] Such labels, though, imply a respect for free-market capitalism that simply cannot be found in *The Servile State*. Rather, Belloc deemed "the capitalist state" both "unstable" and deadly: "If you left men completely free under a capitalist system, there would be so heavy a mortality from starvation as would dry up the sources of labor in a very short time."[3] And he went on to advocate the use of state power, particularly the power of differential taxation, for a dismantling of big corporations, a thorough soaking of the rich, and the massive redistribution of their property to those without any.[4]

Considering that agenda, other biographers have labeled Belloc a kind of socialist.[5] They cast his political-economic agenda as "childishly simple" and attractive primarily to "shaggy William-Morrisy idealists," precursors to the Hippies of the 1960s.[6] In reality, though, Belloc condemned public ownership of property and indicted the political order of early twentieth century Britain for introducing a new kind of slavery into the world.

Such confusion, especially among conservative readers, also attends Richard Weaver's small book, *Ideas Have Consequences*,[7] and for the same reason. The titles of these volumes are wonderfully adaptable to the vacuous form of discourse common to early twenty-first century American conservatism. It seems clear that few contemporary conservative pundits who cite these titles have actually read them; fewer still have understood them. For the key to the two books is a common reading of history and an implicit common agenda. Simply put, both

Belloc and Weaver saw Europe's High Middle Ages (circa A.D. 1250) as the era when human society embodied moral virtue, good order, and social justice; and they saw philosophical nominalism, scientific logic, and capitalism (properly defined) as the modern enemies of the good society.

Belloc insisted that the critical parts, or cells, of this good society were productive families, secure in their property. The whole objective of his political economy was to break down the corruptions of modern capitalism and socialism, and re-establish families in working homes set on land in freehold tenure. His models were the artisans and the free peasants of the High Middle Ages, a community held together by the Christian Church and a religiously infused aristocracy attentive to its duties. To be understood, *The Servile State* must be read through this lens, one rarely used by Tea Party enthusiasts or talk-show pundits.

Building on the Insights of Pope Leo XIII

Hilaire Belloc was clear that the inspiration for his analysis in *The Servile State* was Pope Leo XIII's 1891 encyclical, *Rerum Novarum*. On the one hand, this document was "modern," representing the Roman Catholic Church's readiness to engage—rather than simply denounce—the new urban-industrial age and the place of wage laborers within it. On the other hand, *Rerum Novarum* was "reactionary," for its program aimed at restoring a social-economic order that resembled—in its most important components—the High Middle Ages.

For example, the encyclical was Agrarian in its insistence that all wealth derived from the land: "the earth, even though apportioned among private owners, ceases not thereby to minister to the needs of all, in as much as there is not one who does not sustain life from what the land produces." Even those who possessed no soil contributed their labor. In consequence, "it may truly be said that *all human subsistence is derived either from labor on one's own land, or from some toil, some calling, which is paid for either in the produce of the land itself, or on that which is exchanged for what the land brings forth*."[8]

Leo also affirmed the theory of "labor property," rooted in the "law of nature." He wrote:

> Now, when man thus turns that activity of his mind and the strength of his body toward procuring the fruits of nature, *by such act he makes his own that portion of nature's field which he cultivates*—that portion on which he leaves, as it were, the impress of his personality.

It was "just" that the laborer possess what he had made, and no one had standing to violate that right.[9]

The "natural and original right of marriage" and "the principle purpose of marriage ordained by God's authority from the beginning"—namely, to: "Increase and multiply"—were also linked to the physicality of home, tools, and land: "The right of property . . . must in likewise belong to a man in his capacity of head of a family." Indeed, this right was "all the stronger" as it found "a wider expression in the family group." The ability to pass on resources for survival to children through inheritance was also important: "in no other way can a father affect this except by the ownership of productive property."[10]

It was in this context that Leo rejected "the main tenet of socialism, [the] community of goods," because it "would violate a natural right and introduce confusion and disorder into the commonweal." Indeed, private ownership should "be held sacred and inviolable." However, this meant something other than merely protecting the assets of the relatively few who—circa 1912—actually owned productive property. Rather, as Leo explained, "the law . . . should favor ownership, and its policy should be to induce as many as possible of the people to become owners." This would also be the solution to "the social question" of the age: "If working people can be encouraged to look forward to obtaining a share in the land," then "the gulf between vast wealth and sheer poverty will be bridged over."[11]

The Development of the Capitalist State

Belloc's project in *The Servile State* was to analyze how that "gulf" had emerged, what had been the consequences, and how the elements of a good society might be put back together again. An important component of this task was to reframe history, in order to understand how a system of ordered liberty and widely dispersed property had come to an end. Belloc began the story shortly after the fall of the Western Roman Empire. Between A.D. 500 and 1000, he said, the Christianized Europeans—just like the pagan Romans before them—took slavery for granted. However, slaves were no longer "made" by conquest. Rather, "it was poverty that made the slave," as individuals or families accepted slavery as an alternative to indigence. There was no organized protest against the system based on conscience. Rather, slavery was accepted by owners and slaves alike as an inevitable aspect of the human condition.

The end of European slavery, according to Belloc, came through "the experiment called the Christian church." While no church dogma explicitly condemned slavery, the Christian emphasis on spiritual equality undermined its premises. At a physical level, the emergence of the autonomous villa, or estate, eventually rooted the slave. Over time, an implicit bargain emerged between lord and slave family: the latter would be attached to a particular section of land, would pay the lord a fixed amount of crop (or, later, a customary fee), and would retain the balance for consumption or private sale. By A.D. 900, the buying and selling of men had largely come to an end. About the same time, cities began to re-emerge as trading centers. Craft guilds developed as self-governing efforts to control competition among artisans, assuring good quality, "fair" prices, and secure incomes. Under these circumstances, there could neither be capitalist nor proletarian. Indeed, by A.D. 1250, a well-developed "distributive system" existed in Central and Western Europe (including Britain), with three forms of labor: the serf, secure in his position, who paid regular but limited dues and services fixed by long custom; the freeholder peasant, who related to rulers through taxes; and the guildsman.

All three types of labor also shared in the common property of villages, where rights to graze a cow or gather acorns and firewood were well-defined and zealously protected. This was essentially an agrarian system: "Then, as now, the soil and its fixtures were the basis of all wealth." As Belloc summarized: "all three between them were making for a society which should be based upon the principle of property. *All, or most—the normal family—should own.* And on ownership the freedom of the state should repose." It was true that co-operative bodies, such as guilds and religious fraternities, placed certain restraints on personal economic liberty. However, this was for the preservation of a greater liberty resting on real economic democracy.[12]

The end of the medieval-distributist order came in the sixteenth century, when there arose, according to Belloc, "the dreadful moral anarchy which goes by the name of capitalism." While most economic historians trace the origin of this economic ideology in Britain to the eighteenth century, Belloc insisted that the change was much older. And over three centuries, it transformed Britain from a land of owners into (by 1912) a place where a third of the people was indigent and 95 percent dispossessed of all capital and land.[13]

Capitalism emerged through "the deliberate action of men, *evil will in a few*, and apathy of will among the many." The first stage came in the 1530s, an "artificial revolution of the most violent kind," involving the seizure of monastic lands by King Henry VIII. Prior to this revolution, about a third of England's land belonged to the squires or county lords, a third belonged to free peasants, and a third to church entities. Most of the land that Henry confiscated, as part of his "Reformation," eventually wound up in the hands of the squires, who now emerged as a powerful, effectively uncontrolled economic oligarchy. In the 1640s, this group eliminated the monarchy as a threat to its power. The same small oligarchy controlled Parliament and used Enclosure Acts and a Statute of Frauds to chase free peasants off their customary lands and to seize the village commons for consolidation into corporate-style farms.[14]

Few Property Owners, Many Dispossessed Workers

Reflecting his startling departure from orthodox history, Belloc concluded that by 1700, "England had already become capitalist," with "a vast section of her population" proletarianized. It was this change, he insisted, and not the later Industrial Revolution, "which accounts for the terrible social condition in which we find ourselves today." The introduction of industrial processes—Watt's condensor, Hargrave's spinning jenny, King's flying shuttle—were *not* the causes of monopoly. By the time they appeared, England had already been captured by an oligarchy. If these inventions had arrived in the thirteenth century, Belloc insisted, they "would have blest and enriched mankind" and would have been organized on a cooperative basis. Instead, they fostered still further consolidation through the trusts; such economic combinations brought "the ruin of the smaller competition through secret conspiracies entered into by the larger men, and supported by the secret force of the state."[15]

Socialism emerged in the nineteenth century as a movement to counter the oligarchy. However, "the effect of socialist doctrine upon capitalist society is [actually] to produce a third thing different from either of its two begetters—to wit, the servile state."

This was not meant just as a criticism of the modern welfare state, as many conservatives now suppose. Rather, the Servile State marked "the re-establishment of slavery as a *necessary component of capitalism.*" More specifically, the Servile State existed when ownership of the means of production "by a few" came into "stable equilibrium by the establishment of compulsory labor legally enforceable upon those who do not own the means of production for the advantage of those who do."[16] What did Belloc specifically mean by these claims?

43

He saw capitalist society dividing into two classes: a small member of free citizens who owned productive property and a dispossessed majority who were masters only of their labor and who had no control over capital or land. The Servile State develops as the ownership class and the government converge around the goal of security. In this form of state capitalism, government provides to the free "security" in their property and profits, rent and interest. For the property-less unfree, the government guarantees security in subsistence. In exchange for a surrender of economic autonomy and for acceptance of permanent status as wage-laborers, the unfree gain a minimum wage which provides "sufficiency and security," workmen's compensation insurance which cements a new form of inferior status, and means-tested unemployment and sickness insurance which reinforces their status as proletarians. The inevitable consequence of these measures, Belloc argued, was compulsory labor: the expectation that all unfree adults would be in the wage-labor market. State schooling reinforces the process: "Roughly speaking, it is the generation brought up under the Education Acts of the last forty years which has grown up definitely and hopelessly proletarian."[17] Notably, the children of the unfree learned that property ownership is beyond them; that they must think of themselves as wage-earners alone.

Belloc neatly summarized the new servile order: "Subject the proletarian, as a proletarian, and because he is a proletarian, to special laws. Clothe me, the capitalist, as a capitalist, and because I am a capitalist, with special converse duties under those laws." Laborers accept this surrender "of a mere legal freedom" because the Servile State provides "the very real prospect of having enough and not losing it." Indeed, Belloc acknowledges that in strict terms of material welfare, the newly enslaved may be better off than if they owned property and were responsible for their own support. Partly for this reason, Belloc concluded that the strains of capitalism would relax "and the community will settle down upon the servile basis which was its foundation before the advent of the Christian faith, from what that faith slowly weaned it, and to which in the decay of the faith it naturally returns."[18]

The Distributist Alternative

How might a community escape this end? In *The Servile State*, Belloc offered little practical guidance. The clear alternative was rebuilding a social-economic order featuring widely distributed property. However, "Will man want to own? . . . Can I discover any relics of the cooperative instinct . . .?" Most of the unfree, Belloc mused, seemed content in their servility. Owning property meant bearing responsibility for its protection and maintenance and facing many risks, without guarantee of reward. In comparison, the Servile State offered a meager but secure level of subsistence: a genial form of slavery.[19] Most modern men wanted income, the consumption of cheap, industrial goods, and the security of state welfare, *not* the challenges of property.

It would be in his subsequent *The Restoration of Property* that Belloc laid out a fairly complete distributist program of reform. Family freedom, he said, required "a jealous watch against, and destruction of, monopoly" and "the safeguarding of inheritance, especially the inheritance of small patrimonies." The goal was "a society in which property is well distributed and so large a proportion of the families in the state severally own and therefore control the means of production as to determine the general tone of society." Controversially, Belloc reasoned that since the architects of the Servile State had used law and police powers to build their regime, from Enclosure Acts in the seventeenth and eighteenth centuries to the welfare measures of the early twentieth century, "in this attempt to restore Economic Freedom, the powers of the State must be invoked." This would include protection against "direct rapine" and from "the exaggeration of competition." Guild-like structures should be empowered and official machinery created to foster the propagation of small property.[20]

Regarding specifics, Belloc favored the use of differential taxes to redistribute property. For example, he would tax "chain" retailers so that one company could run no more than a dozen stores. He would handicap department stores, like Harrod's, in a similar way. A "turnover tax" would be imposed on large wholesalers; small, family-held firms would be tax free. Large industrial plants would face a tax on power used; artisans would enjoy protection and subsidized credit. Electricity and the internal combustion engine—both favorable to family-scale production—would be encouraged; steam and water power would be taxed. Agricultural land would be restored to families: "there must be a radical difference in the burdens imposed upon the land occupied, as land (according to our view) should be occupied, *by a human family living thereon*, and land occupied by others from whom the owners draw tribute." State policy should support subsistence farming and "privilege" this peasantry "as against the diseased society around it." Taxes on real estate transactions should "make it easy for the smaller man to buy land from the richer man and difficult for the larger man to buy from the smaller man." Belloc noted that medieval guilds had not entirely disappeared; doctors and lawyers, for example, still maintained guild-like structures that controlled entry into the professions, mandated certain forms of training, and the like. The trade unions, which bore a "proletarian spirit," should be replaced by similar guild structures that again controlled quality, regulated training, and set just prices.[21]

While the sweep of Belloc's public-policy agenda would cause mass heart failure at a modern Tea Party Rally, he insisted that his project was properly labeled reactionary. He sought the method:

> by which a reaction against Capitalism and its product, Communism, may be begun . . . The main task remains not that of elaborating machinery for the reaction toward right living, but of forwarding the spirit of that reaction in a society which has almost forgotten what property and its concomitant freedom means.[22]

Policy Insights

Is *The Servile State*, with its strong whiffs of medievalism, actually relevant to early twenty-first century America? The answer is yes. Certainly, the financial crisis of 2008 and its consequences underscored the reality and perils of a servile economy. The vast majority of Americans put their faith in wages, retirement accounts resting on stocks and bonds, and the government safety net. Faith in all three was shaken by subsequent events, just as Belloc would have predicted. Jobs were lost; the decline in real wages—evident since the 1970s—accelerated. Individual Retirement Accounts proved to be fragile, ephemeral forms of private property; as the old saying went, you can't eat a stock certificate. And the government safety net revealed many holes, sure to become wider and more numerous as lawmakers dealt with yawning federal and state budget deficits.

All the same, was not the "housing bubble" the cause of the panic of 2008? And was it not a consequence, in turn, of the distributist goal of delivering widespread home ownership? Could not Belloc's very scheme be indicted as the cause of recent economic woes?

If still alive, Belloc would probably give three answers. First, he never claimed that everyone should own property. Even under the best of cultural circumstances, many were unfit to bear the responsibilities involved. He certainly would not have approved of issuing mortgages to persons without the means to pay for them. Second, Belloc would have objected to the very nature of the modern American housing market. Laws favoring home ownership should have the purpose of settling families in proper structures and building stable communities. In America, however, home ownership has become in large measure a method of speculative investment. This is the very antithesis of distributist principles. And third, Belloc would have stressed that distributists never sought *just* home ownership. The goal was to places families in *productive* homes, with small workshops, loom rooms, food preservation facilities, chicken coops, and gardens as the norm. Today, he would have added home offices, computer rooms, home-schooling rooms, and so on. The typical American suburban home—commonly prohibited by zoning laws and restrictive covenants from housing *any* kind of work—is simply not part of the distributist vision.

From Aristotle to Thomas Jefferson to contemporary writers such as Wendell Berry, the linkage of property ownership and a vital home economy to true liberty and security has endured as a basic political vision. Whereas raw capitalism ends up in an unholy alliance with collectivism known as the Servile State, the distributism of Hilaire Belloc would deliver an economy fit for families. Far from being just a reactionary medievalist, Belloc may actually represent the most prescient of analysts and guides to a sustainable and child-rich future.

Notes

1. Robert Nisbet, "Introduction," in *The Servile State*, ed. Hilaire Belloc (Indianapolis, IN: Liberty Classics, 1977 [1912]), 18.
2. Joseph Pearce, *Old Thunder: A Life of Hilaire Belloc* (New York: Harper Collins, 2002), 195.
3. Belloc, *The Servile State*, 114.
4. The full policy implications of *The Servile State* are drawn out in: Hilaire Belloc, *The Restoration of Property* (New York: Sheed and Ward, 1936).
5. Robert Speaight, *The Life of Hilaire Belloc* (London: Hollis & Canter, 1957), 317.
6. A.N. Wilson, *Hilaire Belloc* (London: Hamish Hamilton, 1984), 292–94.
7. Richard Weaver, *Ideas Have Consequences* (Chicago, IL: University of Chicago Press, 1948).
8. Pope Leo XIII, *Rerum Novarum* [May 1891]; from http://www.vatican.va/holy_father/leo_xiii/encyclicals/documents/hf_1-xiii_enc_1505189. . . [accessed 11/27/2006], 3.
9. Leo XIII, *Rerum Novarum*, 4 (emphasis added).
10. Ibid.
11. Ibid, 5, 12, 14
12. Belloc, *The Servile State*, 64–81, 87 (emphasis added).
13. Ibid, 82.
14. Ibid, 82–94 (emphasis added).
15. Ibid, 96–102, 117.
16. Ibid, 32, 35, 39.

17. Ibid, 48–61, 155, 174–84.
18. Ibid, 143, 161, 198.
19. Ibid, 131–33.
20. Belloc, *The Restoration of Property*, 17, 28, 35.
21. Ibid, 67–73, 90, 107, 113, 116, 137.
22. Ibid, 144.

5

Bard of the Wapsipinicon: Jay G. Sigmund

The past fifteen years have witnessed a modest revival of interest in the work of poet, dramatist, and fiction writer Jay G. Sigmund, Iowa's "forgotten regionalist." The revival began with E. Bradford Burns' splendid history published in 1996, *Kinship with the Land: Regionalist Thought in Iowa, 1894–1942*. The first phrase in the title came from a 1925 Sigmund poem and the volume's frontispiece featured Sigmund's "Morning Mists on the Wapsipinicon," one of his most representative verses. Burns openly agreed with the 1930 judgment of John T. Frederick, editor of the Iowa City-based literary journal *The Midland*, that "[i]f I were asked to mention a writer in whose work I find fully represented all that is racy and authentic in Iowa life, all that is specifically Iowan, I would think of Sigmund at once."[1] It was followed in 2008 by Zachary Michael Jack's *The Plowman Sings: The Essential Fiction, Poetry, and Drama of America's Forgotten Regionalist Jay G. Sigmund*. It featured an able introductory essay and a solid selection from Sigmund's writings. Jack concluded that his subject's influence peaked in the decade after 1927, when Sigmund "lived at the heart of the Regionalist movement, mentored the next generation of Iowa writers [notably Paul Engle of the Iowa Writers Workshop fame] . . . and brought the literary attentions of the nation back to Iowa."[2]

Finally, in 2011, Sigmund's first collection of poems, *Frescoes*, also came back into print.[3]

Jay Sigmund is part of that rarefied circle of widely published American poets who are also successful businessmen. In the last hundred years, only two other poets—Wallace Stevens and Dana Gioia—would probably join Sigmund there.

All the same, Sigmund remains relatively unknown, particularly among scholars and readers of a traditionalist bent. Moreover, important aspects of his story are still unexamined. In this chapter, I will explore several of these, including: his transition from free verse to formal poetic forms; his effort to escape the confining label of "businessman-poet"; his pleasantly reactionary interpretation of American history, particularly of European settlers and the Indians; his idiosyncratic iconoclasm (as found in the "Bartender Poems"); his post-1930 economic populism, peculiar for a prominent corporate leader; and his telling fascination, as a Protestant, for all things Catholic.

Child of Waubeek

Born December 11, 1885, Jay Sigmund spent his boyhood on a tenant farm near Waubeek, in East-Central Iowa. "The soil of the farm was sandy and thin," he reported, and almost all of his subsequent "farm" poetry and stories featured people struggling to eke out a living on this marginal Iowa land.

The village of Waubeek drew its name from Longfellow's poem, "Hiawatha." It was said to be an Indian word for limestone boulders. The Wapsipinicon River flowed by, carving out limestone bluffs and caves on its way, and capturing young Sigmund's imagination. "There is no more beautiful country than the vicinity around Waubeek," he always said.

He attended a small country school, and developed an early affection for natural history.[4] Given his son's distaste for farming, the elder Sigmund considered the boy an idler; he clearly preferred fishing, hunting, and collecting Indian pottery, arrowheads, and legends.[5] All his life, Jay Sigmund roamed the woods near Waubeek, gathering berries and mushrooms.[6]

In 1895, the family left the farm, moving into the village. At age 14, Sigmund acquired a book on taxidermy; his high school soon had "quite a little museum of mounted birds and animals." Partway through the tenth grade, though, Sigmund left school, ending his formal education.[7]

He moved to nearby Cedar Rapids, and worked for three years at a wholesale grocery. Sigmund began to write at this time, sending "an occasional bit of reporting" to a Chicago theatrical magazine. He also submitted a short story to *Black Cat Magazine*; the editor quickly rejected it. In 1907, the gregarious young man joined the Cedar Rapids Life Insurance Company, beginning "a long and rather strenuous struggle to get a foothold in the business of life insurance salesmanship." In fact, he proved to be a natural. Not only did he quickly rise into "The $100,000 Club" [today's Million Dollar Roundtable], he also wrote a course for his company on how to sell life insurance. The ten lessons included: "Over the Grade—A Dangerous Age"; "Oh! Have You Gone Into the Life Insurance Business?", and "Master of the Situation." In 1924, he became vice-president, board member, and agency manager for the company.[8]

While most literary figures in the 1920s strove to gain bohemian credentials, Jay Sigmund lived a very conventional, and fully bourgeois life. In 1910, he married Louise B. Hearns of Cedar Rapids; they would have a son and two daughters. His wife was the consummate home-maker, gaining some notice for her cooking. The Sigmund country cottage on the Wapsipinicon eventually won fame among the literati for down home Iowa cooking. For example, two visiting New York food editors praised Mrs. Sigmund's menu of pot roast, potato pancakes, yellow butter mushrooms "gathered in the field and sprinkled with caraway seeds as they cooked," and peach dumpling. No can opener was involved, "unless you count the 267 quarts of food stuff, not including jams, jellies and pickles, canned by Mrs. Sigmund last summer."[9] After eating at the Sigmund cottage, *Saturday Review of Literature* co-founder Christopher Morley declared that "Iowa will not produce any great works of art until its diet of hot biscuits and chicken gravy is changed, because no one can maintain that spiritual unease and somberness necessary to the creative faculty after such a meal."[10]

Jay Sigmund was also fully engaged as a civic leader. He served as President of the Cedar Rapids Art Association, a member of the Linn County Social Welfare Board, a member of the Cedar Rapids Public Library Board, and on the Play Selection Committee for the Community Players. Leaving behind a low-church evangelical past, Jay Sigmund and family were staunch members of the very respectable Grace Episcopal Church.[11]

In addition, Sigmund developed an important friendship with Cedar Rapids artist Grant Wood. They became acquainted during the 1920s. Zachary Michael Jack credits the insurance executive with encouraging Wood to abandon his early, imitative French impressionism in favor of the "beauties of Iowa."[12] When Grant Wood held his famous summer art colony at Stone City, the artists in residence would put on a variety show Sunday afternoons to raise money to cover expenses. Jay Sigmund served as the master of ceremonies.[13] In August 1933, Sigmund suffered a serious auto accident, which left him with a crippled right hand. Wood immortalized the event in his painting, "Ridge Road Accident." In June 1935, Grant Wood and wife moved into "a little house in Waubeek" and Sigmund anticipated seeing them "every day . . . through August."[14]

Amateur Versifier

While moving ahead in business and domestic life, Sigmund's real passion became writing. In 1921, he submitted a poem, "Birds of Prey," to Milwaukee's *American Poetry Magazine*. "To my utter amazement," he later wrote, "they accepted the poem and printed it." In consequence:

> I became an incurable amateur versifier, and began to devote most of my spare time to the study of poetry and the writing of it. In fact, it became my hobby, supplanting golf, baseball, bridge, billiards and all the other things which the majority of men care for.[15]

Mixing business and hobby, Sigmund wrote another poem—"Twilight Years"—for *The Underwriters' Review*. Over the next few years, he also had poems published in *The Lyric* (Norfolk, Virginia), *The Reviewer* (Richmond, Virginia), *Sports Afield* (Chicago), *The Lyric West* (Los Angeles), *The Midland* (Iowa City), *The Overland* (San Francisco), *The Country Bard* (Madison, New Jersey), *The Modern Review* (Boston), *The Pagan* (New York), *The Chicago News*, and *The Cincinnati Star-Times*.

William Stanley Braithwaite, a prominent anthologist of magazine and newspaper poetry, urged Sigmund in 1922 to collect his poems in a volume. The result was *Frescoes*. The best of these were odes to birds: Osprey, Pigeon, Robin, Cardinal, and Humming Bird. "To a Goldfinch" was representative:

> Are you a tiny fragment
> Of some yellow moon,
> Carelessly tossed down to earth
> With your cheery tune?[16]

Many of the other selections, though, were imitative, over-written, and in free verse. "The Athenian" deals with a Greek shoe-shine boy. Referring to Socrates, Plato, and Diogenes, Sigmund asks: "Does the blood of these / Flow also in his veins?" In "Father of Waters," the poet ponders the Mississippi River with a "quaking fright": ". . . perhaps more as a child stands dumbly / At sight of his first Christmas-tree / Or a blaring circus parade." Several deal with troubled women: "The Serpent," about a "sexless spinster" given to gossip; and "The Drudge" about an abused farm wife: "ugly, misshapen, shriveled, and faded / I struggle on."[17]

And yet, Sigmund was painfully aware of his lack of formal education and of training in writing. In the many talks that he gave to students and civic groups, he commonly cast doubt on his status. "I'm not sure whether I deserve classification as a poet," he told his audience at a business school in Mason City. "I'm not sure whether I've ever written a line of poetry."[18] While few specifics are known, he clearly read widely in contemporary poetry and fiction, striving to improve his craft. For example, he "followed closely . . . for years" the work of D. H. Lawrence[19] and carefully studied T. S. Eliot's "Murder in the Cathedral."[20] While never quite saying so, Sigmund seemed intent on escaping the freak status of "businessman-poet," seeking acceptance as a writer alone.

During 1922 and 1923, he largely abandoned free verse, turning to conventional poetic forms of rhythm and rhyme. Sigmund grew particularly fond of the sonnet. As the budding Iowa novelist Ruth Suckow wrote on reading the second volume of his verse: "It seems to me that some of the poems, particularly those in regular verse form, are better than those in your first volume."[21] All the same, there remained a forced quality to his poetry. Sigmund was downcast when New Mexican poet Arthur Davison Ficke took him to task for some awkward rhymes. Sigmund asked whether he should stop writing. Ficke urged him to continue working, but clarified: "I only meant that it was important that you realize to what an extent you are, at present, the slave of your rhymes." He suggested that Sigmund "always look ahead," and not decide on the first rhyme-word until he had at least some idea of what the second would be.[22] Whether or not he found this advice useful, Sigmund's versifying steadily improved over the remaining years of the 1920s.

Another reason for this improvement was his decision to focus completely on the Wapsipinicon Valley and its environs. Sigmund, who apparently never traveled further from Iowa than Chicago, simply brought his art home. As he explained, long before this became the mantra of "creative writing" teachers everywhere: "Poetry is not a thing of far places. You can see it, you can find it right at hand." He held that "poetry exists in the daily living of a life" and that rhythm "is the great scheme of things present even in our pulse." All locales could yield their "overtones if one is sensitive enough to register them."[23]

Ruth Suckow was correct. Sigmund's second collection of poems, *Pinions*, was a considerable improvement over his first. Its themes were fresh; its language original; its poetic forms more traditional. There were "bird poems" again, supplemented this time by a series of "Corn-Belt Village Portraits," all written in Iowa dialect. Another favored subject was the changing of the seasons, such as "February":

> The dainty cedar waxwing
>   In her bonnet, nun-like . . . plain . . .
> Now yearns for cherry luncheons
>   And for balmy April's rain!
> Few bards have touched their lyres
>   For this month, but I shall sing—
> Praising its weeping snow-men
>   For it paves the path to spring![24]

Land O'Maize Folks, a third collection, appeared in 1924 and included twenty-five poems on "Mississippi River Village Folk." Mostly light and humorous, "The Old Ferryman Speaks" was typical:

> There was Pat Bender's wife
> Run off with Abner Ross;
> They got me out of bed
> And I rowed them across.
> Just four days after that
> I brought her back to Pat!

Sigmund was also emerging as a master at capturing the moods of the Wapsipinicon landscape. This from "Marsh Road":

> Comes night . . . I'm grateful
>   for the firefly
>   and thin slice of moon! . . .
> For dark brings witch talk,
>   from the pied frog
>   and chortling loon.
>
> I urge my slow feet
>   toward that lamp-light
>   on yon hill's crest.
> Ghost shadows gambol
>   along the marsh road—

Jay Sigmund continued to display, as well, a deft touch in capturing the subtleties of human character. "A Maize Country's Pioneer's Internment" skillfully revealed the distinctive mind of the authentic farmer:

> There in a vase close to his sunken cheek,
> They have placed blossoms, bathed with dew this morn—
> Flowers to him were weeds—did none bring corn—
> One stalk of wheat—a wisp of bearded rye
> Or anything which pleased his living eye?[25]

In 1925, Sigmund published *Drowsy Ones*. The title came from an old school history: "And they called this land, 'Iowa,' which is the Indian name for 'Drowsy Ones'"—this, a far superior translation compared to the banal "Beautiful Land" commonly used today. In "Visitor," he recorded the meeting of a farmer with an old friend who had moved to the city. Raising classic agrarian themes, the latter spoke:

> For he had kept deep-rooted in the clay
>   While I had chosen market-place and street;
>   I knew the city's bricks would bruise his feet
> And send him soon to go his plodding way. . . .
>
> Then I who long had pitied peasant folk
>   And broken faith with field and pasture ground.
>   Felt dull and leaden-footed in my round
> And strangely like a cart-beast with a yoke!

As in the earlier volumes, Sigmund gave frequent attention to the place of women in his valley. Some of these poems were unconventional; this from "Cross-Roads Magdalene":

> So when they made the grocer's son admit
>   That he had found her lovecraft ripe and whole,
>   They hated him because he dared to take
>   The fruit that each had yearned for in his heart
>   The very thing they knew they could not have:
> Then they expressed concern about her soul!

More common was verse that explored the burdens and fantasies of the farm wife. From "Prairie Wife's Wage":

> The somber sleeper at her side—
>   A jungle king with burning eyes;
> The houseplants on her windowsill
>   Are orchid blooms of giant size.
>
> That cradle, rocking back and forth,
>   May seem to her as jade and gold:
> The peas she hulled were deep sea pearls—
>   As many as her hand could hold.[26]

Around 1921, Jay Sigmund joined the English Club at Cornell College, in nearby Mt. Vernon. He regularly attended club meetings and dinners, read his verse, and encouraged student writers. The club's journal, *The Husk*, featured Sigmund's work in its March 1929 issue. "Craftswoman" returned to the peculiar, but real satisfactions of farm wives:

> I stepped upon a braided span
>> Her subtle finger-skill had made—
> A prayer-rug for a kneeling man,
>> So delicate the weave and shade
>
> "My wedding gown is there". . . .
>
> Beauty had brushed my soul that day,
>> Beauty the wild, elusive moth,
> And the bent old-wife had shown the way
>> Beauty can be in attic cloth.[27]

The powerful bond of the soil's fecundity to human fertility emerged in another poem written for The English Club, "Firstborn":

> Fecund the land; oats ready for binning
>> And in the house the midwife's watchful eye
> Waiting to find the signs of life beginning—
>> Waiting to catch firstborn's treble cry. . . .
>
> Hoping his tired mate would cease her labors—
>> Soon give another life to fight the soil,
> So the midwife's tongue could tell the curious neighbors—
>> Life; life; birth; death; green sod; more lives; more toil.[28]

"Life of the People"

In addition to encouraging Sigmund as a poet, novelist Ruth Suckow was probably responsible, at least in part, for Jay Sigmund's turn to writing short fiction. In a note to him dated September 4, 1923, she advised: "You have a deft touch with character, which makes me wonder if after all you wouldn't prefer prose to verse."[29] His first published stories appeared within a year. Sigmund later explained that in his fiction, he tried to do:

> . . . this one thing: To take the commonplace materials that lie at hand here in Iowa and weave them into stories—not commercial stories, but stories that will depict the life of the people here at home as they go about their every-day rounds with something of accuracy and as honestly as I can.[30]

While some of his poetry displayed romantic agrarian themes, almost all of Sigmund's short fiction was gritty, hard. As Suckow had noted, Sigmund was skilled at creating characters. Even in stories no more than three or four pages in length, he conveyed images and descriptions so well that readers could feel they know each central character's whole life story. As Burns relates, Sigmund's prose was "spare, precise, [and] somber." He continued: "A touch of irony, much folk wisdom, a healthy dose of wry humor, and a dash of pathos pervade the tightly woven, well-constructed stories."[31]

Sigmund's first prose collection appeared in 1927. Entitled *Wapsipinicon Tales*, the volume featured an Introduction by Newberry award-winning author Charles Finger. He praised Sigmund for providing "the romance of the commonplace," stories "of people of no importance; of the meek who inherit the earth; of workaday men who are anything but brilliant and dashing."[32] Characteristic was the story, "Blinkers," a fascinating account of the illegal cock-fighting circuit in rural Iowa, told by a one-eyed Civil War veteran. He describes an upcoming contest between the line-bred cocks from Ireland, "Whitehackles," and the cross-bred cocks from the Orient, "Rattlesnakes." On the appointed day, "[e]ven the sheriff and a district-court judge was there in the crowd. Of course in them days if an official had dared to interfere with a cock fight he'd never get elected again."[33]

A second collection, *Merged Blood*, appeared two years later. Among these stories was "Dubbing Season," another recounting of fighting fowls. This time, a city matron from the Humane Society accidentally discovers hunter and trapper Alva Whitefield, illegally cutting off the combs and lobes of a young gamecock. The sheriff arrives the next day, urging him to plead guilty and pay a fine. A lament over the passing of rural ways follows, one strangely relevant to our own heavily regulated world: "'Pa said the time would come someday when they'd arrest a man for even keepin' game chickens,' muttered Alva to himself. 'I didn't believe it.'" Another solid tale, "Testimony," focuses on an old German immigrant with a bad heart, Henry Fehrling. He turns for relief to a patent medicine, and becomes obsessed by the wonderful printed testimonials of the "many who had been snatched from the very jaws of death by Dr. Johnson's marvelous medicine." He yearns to "knock at the door of this happy fraternity, for admission," and laboriously writes his own testimonial, which he submits. Weeks later, he is thrilled when a new advertisement reports, "Middle Western farmer is cured of heart trouble!" In the text which followed, "[m]any of the words were not spelled as Henry had spelled them and it seemed to him a certain power had been instilled into his sentences as well as a fairsized paragraph added." Still, his joy is complete . . . until he collapses from heart failure.[34]

Jay Sigmund's art reached a high point in 1930 with the publication of *The Ridge Road*. It contained six stories appearing for the first time and fifteen poems. Several of them would win awards that year. The best story, in my view, was "Balm," an uncharacteristically tender and sweet tale. It comes from the mouth of a twelve-year-old boy, recently orphaned, who has been taken in by a young, childless couple, Julius and Mag. Julius had been a "rough fellow" raised in the French Ridge Settlement, but "Ma said he changed when he got married." After morning chores, the three set out for a picnic and an afternoon of fishing on the Wapsipinicon. The story recounts the banter of the day, as the couple draws the boy into their family circle. After catching a basket of fish, for example, Julius cleans and fries them in a skillet:

> The fish beat any I'd ever had, and I told Julius so.
> "I'm some cook, ain't I Dick," Julius said.
> I told him I thought so.
> "If Mag gets mad at us and leaves, we'll get
> along all right, won't we?"
> I didn't say anything, but Mag laughed and then
> we all laughed."

Later, after releasing several more hooked fish, Julius declares, "We'll get them next summer, Dick." And the boy thinks: "Somehow it made me feel good to hear Julius planning fun for him and me together next summer."[35]

Among the poems, a long dark tale—"Three Women and a Man"— stands out. It tells of a bachelor farmer, successful but lonely, who finds a young woman in town to marry. He "felt a new pride in his oatfield hill," but was crushed when she died in childbirth. After several years of bitter widowhood, he marries a recently widowed neighbor, who moves in with her nearly grown daughter, one who had "the cold face of a nun." He soon senses that matters are awry, as the two "whispered when they heard him swing the gate" and exchanged looks which made him uneasy. He would retreat outside at night:

> But when there came a short lull in the sounds,
> He heard vague whisperings within his house—

Voices that scratched the silence like a mouse
Which gnaws the rafters in his midnight rounds.

During Spring planting, the farmer takes a chill and develops pneumonia. The women provide him indifferent care, and he dies, a victim of "whispered plans now all complete."[36]

Discovered

By this time, Sigmund had been "discovered." California poet Robinson Jeffers, reading *Drowsy Ones*, replied: "You have fine powers of observation and imaginative sympathy, as well as a musical verse, and you see keenly and objectively."[37] Louis Mumford published several of Sigmund's poems in *The Caravan*, and commented: "Your poetry gives one a rich and satisfactory sense of the mid-American earth, and I rejoice in it."[38] "You have the touch, the color; you see character and present it without dawdling with wasteful words," wrote humorist Opie Read, editor of *The Arkansas Traveler*.[39] Sigmund met Carl Sandburg through Cornell College, where the latter regularly lectured. Sandburg commented that *Wapsipinicon Tales* "delivers the universal thru Iowa and you"; a later collection of stories had "the color of earth as it sifts through the small town."[40] And Count Olya Tolstoy, son of the great Russian novelist, praised the complex truths found in Sigmund's seemingly simple stories, adding: "Contrary to many American writers you are absolutely free from the 'rubber stamp' and I am happy to welcome in you The American Chekoff [sic] and Maupassant."

Anthologists of the "Year's Best" poems and stories also included Sigmund's work in their lists. Regarding his verse, William Stanley Braithwaite's *Eleventh Annual Anthology of Magazine Verse* declared three of the Iowan's poems as "distinctive," including "To a Nesting Robin." It began:

Through new-green elm leaves
Your jet bead eyes
Peer with their searching glances
To measure my size.[41]

The National Country Bard Association [!] voted his poem "Foresight" the "most country-bardy" in its Autumn 1925 competition.[42] *Literary Digest* chose two of Sigmund's poems for inclusion in *The Best Poems of 1926*, published by Dodd, Mead, and Co. One of these was "Surcease":

Now comes a little span when farmers rest,
    Before the new corn shows each pale, green hill
Before the rank weeds anchor choking root
    And fling their poison shade to blight and kill.

And horses, out to pasture on a knoll,
    Show broad, white bands across the shoulders now.
Where sweat and froth beneath each harness strap,
    Gathered like seafoam as they dragged the plow.[43]

In 1931, Jay Sigmund won the prestigious Gypsy Poetry Prize for "Phantom Horses" (the judge was Irish poet George Russell, who wrote as "A. E."). It began:

After the midnight hour has tolled,
    The phantom horses tread the paves
After the last steel wheel has rolled,
    There falls the hooves of saddled slaves.

A mottled mount has gone this way—
    I heard the iron calks strike fire:
A reckless rider reined his bay
    Down where the roadside trees loom higher.

Galloping through the night's black span,
    After the ribboned trail is clear,
There must have been a headless man,
    Rattling a silvered bridle near.[44]

Celebrated as he was for his verse, Sigmund also won praise for his fiction. British anthologist Edward J. O'Brien became one of Jay Sigmund's leading boosters. O'Brien's list of "The Best Stories of 1930," appearing in *The Boston Transcript*, featured *six* pieces by Sigmund ("Trot Lines," "Broken Pump," "Trade," "Blasphemy," "The Hills," and "Lady Slippers"), and four by fellow Iowan Ruth Suckow. His *The Best Short Stories of 1931*, published by Dodd, Mead, carried three of Sigmund's stories from *The Ridge Road* and a similar number by Suckow. O'Brien concluded, with perhaps a bit of overstatement:

Two generations ago Boston was the geographical center of American literary life, one generation ago New York could claim pride of place, and I trust that the idea will not seem too unfamiliar if I suggest that the geographical center today is Iowa City.[45]

During the early 1930s, Sigmund also began to write plays, mostly "One Acts" suitable for amateur companies. He sent one of these,

The Ghoul, to Betty Smith for review. Trained at The Yale University School of Drama and with a number of successful Broadway productions already to her credit, Smith had taken a post as Playwright in Residence for The WPA Federal Theater Project, a New Deal initiative. (In the 1940s, she wrote the best-selling, semi-autobiographical *A Tree Grows in Brooklyn*.) Smith also ran a small business on the side, rewriting other people's drafts for $10 a play. Her response to Sigmund's submission was different, though. "The play is a natural comedy," she wrote. "The plot is better than average, the situations are fine, the people are perfect and the dialogue excellent." While *The Ghouls* had faults, they were minor. "The main thing, *the thing that cannot be taught, is there*." She called him "a natural-born playwright" who lacked nothing "but the little tricks of putting over your work." Instead of a "rewrite," she proposed that they co-author his plays, a fifty-fifty collaboration: "I rewrite your play without charge; submit it wherever I have contacts. If it is sold, the proceeds are to be divided evenly." If no sale after six months, Sigmund had full rights to the play.[46] Over the next twelve months, this partnership saw The Samuel French Company publish "The Tree of His Father," "Folk Stuff," and "Vine Leaves." T. S. Denison and Company published "The Saints Together."[47]

From Virile Pioneers and Boy Scouts to "Starkly Stated Horrors"

Beyond these signs of achievement and recognition—rare for a part-time, "hobbyist" writer—Jay Sigmund's work showed distinctive qualities that deserve attention. Among these was his reactionary understanding of American history, a trait that he shared with other regionalists.

As in Donald Davidson's *Tennessee*, Sigmund portrays the whites who drove off the Indians and settled Iowa in glowing, positive ways. There are no cringing apologies here. *Pinions* included the poem "Corn Country Paean":

> Wide-eyed, the sullen-visaged Sac and Sioux,
> Watched the robed priest and virile sons of soil
> On their chaste prairies—strong of faith set foot—
> To bless with crucifix and sweating toil.

Even the shaggy buffalo seemed "to sense that their fast-thinning ranks / Must pass, to make room for the patient ox." Summoning divine providence, Sigmund continued:

On marched the solemn pageant of the years,
Each with its blessings from the lap of God;
'Til now a people mighty in their strength—
At last have risen from the virgin sod![48]

On other occasions, Sigmund amplified the language of strength to describe the triumph of the white men over the red. Commemorating a country Iowa church, he wrote in "Jordan's Grove":

Here, where the eagle built her nest
   The strong men slept by firelight
And weary women sunk to rest,
   Glad of the silence of the night. . . .

Here, where the bison once fled by,
   The strong men built a shrine to pray
And under God's own curving sky
   They knelt the humble fieldman's way.[49]

Complementing the portrait of the white pioneers was an equally romantic portrait of Iowa's "noble savages," the Sac, Iowa, Fox, and Sioux tribes. This, too, was a theme common to regionalist writers of the early twentieth century.[50] Sigmund thrilled in particular over the legend of the Wapsipinicon, which he told with his own spin. In his version, Wapsi was the daughter of the chief of the Foxes, who met by some fate with Pinicon, son of the chief of the Iowas. Their love was bitterly opposed by their fathers, but they held frequent trysts at night along the beautiful river which divided the tribes' hunting grounds. Wapsi's father caught them one evening, and forbade further meetings. The two formed a suicide pact, and they leapt from a limestone cliff to their death in the river below. In their memory, this body of water became the Wapsipinicon.[51]

Another, more historically authentic tale that fascinated Sigmund was that of Anamosa. This "Indian princess" came one night to the frontier Iowa town of Lexington, and settled there. On her death, the town took her name (notably, Grant Wood would be buried in Anamosa Cemetery). Of her, Sigmund wrote:

Oh, lithe White Fawn, the mystic spell you gave
Has wakened men and cheered them at their toil.
May giant white oaks bend above your grave
With spreading tender ferns to shade the soil.[52]

These views, which would have been considered brazen and politically incorrect in more recent times, also highlight Sigmund's association with the Boy Scouts of America. The local Council maintained Camp Waubeek only a few miles northwest of Sigmund's beloved village. He spent a considerable time at the camp each summer, teaching the Scouts about Indian lore and birds, and leading hikes in the river valley. Sigmund also wrote a number of poems for the Camp, all of which sought to convey the romance of his river to the boys. These lines come from "Council Rock Song":

> Down near the caves where the redmen stayed
> (There are broken vessels to prove the place)
> I saw the ghost of an Indian maid
> But the river mists obscured her face.
>
> I found this feather upon the bar
> (This proves her lover was near that night).
> I heard a paddle . . . I saw a star—
> The mood was mine . . . the setting right. . . .
>
> There is the stream that holds it all—
> Secrets of lovers and fighting ones;
> Here are the Waubeeks, stark and tall—
> Guard this valley and dream, my sons.[53]

Sigmund authored a "poetic legendary drama," "The Wapsipinicon," which told the story of the doomed Indian lovers. Written entirely in verse, the play oozes with overwrought rhymes and sentimentality.[54] Then again, it was not written for hardened New York critics, but for the Boy Scouts. Annual productions had the action taking place on the river and the banks of the Wapsipinicon opposite Camp Waubeek.[55]

This same writer, though, produced other poems and stories with a harsh naturalism that rivaled even figures such as Jack London. In its review of *The Ridge Road*, the British journal *Poetry and the Play* emphasized Sigmund's "stark realism." It continued: ". . . to read Mr. Sigmund is to be introduced to the actualities of a hard and narrow life which is not without heroism."[56] Chicago literary critic Keith Preston argued that "Jay Sigmund does the kind of stuff that is hailed as genius in Scandinavian or Russian realists and ignored for the most part in our national writers."[57] Arthur Davison Ficke cited the "starkly stated horrors" found in many of Sigmund's poems, yet concluded: "I do not see what it is possible for a poet to do nowadays except stick to a bitter honesty such as yours."[58] Poems of particular force included: "Killers," with vivid images of a slaughter house;[59] "Loam-Wounded" and "Second Marriage" from *The Ridge Road*; and "County Home Farmer" from Sigmund's last collection of verse, *Heron at Sunset*.[60]

Also in tension with the ethos of Scouting was Jay Sigmund's iconoclasm toward prevailing forms of American piety. As he wrote in "Tempted":

> My irreproachable family
> (All of them deceased),
> And my physician
> (A most learned individual)
> Together with my pastor
> (A saintly scholar),
> Have warned me often
> Against most of the things
> For which
> I have felt any real attraction.

Yet, when his physician dies at age forty and his pastor is implicated in a "horrid scandal," the poet resolves: "Today / I have a mind / To begin / To enjoy life."[61] In *The Ridge Road*, Sigmund lamented the failures of the young:

> The grizzled ridge road men agree
>   The younger ones are soft these days:
> They cannot hew a helve or yoke—
>   They even sin the softer ways.[62]

Frequently, Sigmund condemned Iowa's strict "Blue Laws," which closed everything down on the Sabbath. Most notably, his *Land O'Maize Folks* contained ten poems (under the label "Yesteryear Folk") praising bartenders and lamenting Prohibition. This section opens with a quotation from Omar Khayyam: "I often wonder what the vintners buy, One half so precious as the goods they sell." Representative of Sigmund's verse was "Bill M' Kellum," which tells of a fellow arriving at the bar on a cold March day, with only a dime in his pocket:

> Bill must have had the gift
> Of second sight;
> He saw my need for grog—
> "Well, Jack," says he,
> "It's almost time for me to

Go off watch:
I wonder if you'll
Take a shot on me!"
He poured us both a slug
Of Joel B.![63]

In a concluding poem, Sigmund admitted that saloons were bad:

Yet, I won't think of them
As dens of vice:
To me they always seemed
Like pilgrim's shrines
Where kindred spirits
Met to swap advice. . . .[64]

The great German–American journalist H. L. Mencken was particularly moved by these poems. "The tales of Gus and Bill positively reduced me to tears," he wrote to Sigmund. "Ah, for the good old days! I knew every bartender in Baltimore."[65]

Another discordant theme in Sigmund's work was his economic and political populism, a strange trait for a man of business. As early as *Pinions*, Sigmund took potshots at the industrialists and bankers:

Please pause a moment, Mr. Bagg O' Gold
Say, what of all these children bending low o'er
    Loom and wheel? . . .
And what of these hearth-stones long gone cold?[66]

And in "Whistles—Seven A.M.," there are lines that could have been penned by the British Distributists Chesterton or Belloc:

It marks the beginning of King Time Clock's day—
Calling to serf-dom a grotesque array
Of puppets. . . . with harsh metal notes[67]

Borrowing, it seems probable, from William Jennings Bryan, Sigmund increasingly employed the images of gathering usurers and the "debtor's cross." In "Corn Country Magnificat," a farmer looks to the probable fate of his new son:

At last the usurers will toss
    Their dice and curse my son:
His loss will merely be their loss—
    His cross is but a debtor's cross.[68]

Such imagery swelled into a powerful poem, "Christ of the Ridgeroad," where Sigmund retold the Passion Story, with a bankrupt farmer as the Christ figure:

> ... Year after year of fruitless furrow toil
> Has shackled him; a Pilate found his field
> And as the usurers demanded all
> The Pilate saw the cattle in his stall
>
> The debtors cross was ready. No respite
> for him; the usurers who made the mob
> Crowed like jackals: 'We are in the right;'
> The drought and sandstorms aided in the job.[69]

Sigmund's last verse collection, *Heron at Sunset*, focused on the plight of Iowa farmers then caught in the depths of the Great Depression. Themes included the new wave of foreclosures, the triumph of cruel economic forces over human dreams, and—again—"the timbers for a debtor's cross." In "New Master—Old Farm," Sigmund explains:

> The new master of these acres knows
> That many owners have come on ahead
> And never whipped these knolls; and so it goes—
> Plow; plant; six feet of earth; a long-time dead.[70]

In "Foreclosed," Sigmund defined a grave as "a loam that has no mortgage"; as one critic correctly put it, such "vehemence" was "unbecoming a life insurance company's vice-president."[71] His strongest image and most forceful cadence came in "Asylum Dance," a portrait of the madness that had claimed some of those who "once possessed a share / Of wide green pastures":

> The screechy fiddle calls the dancers in,
> Joy is not only for the favored few
> Out in the bigger world; begin, begin
> You dying puppets; this night is for you. ...[72]

"Things Catholic"

The most intriguing aspect of Jay Sigmund's work was his deep fascination with Roman Catholicism, particularly the monastic orders. Here too, though, the specific focus of his attention was local.

Sigmund appears to have been born into fundamentalist, "Full Gospel" rural Protestantism. Certainly, he knew the "revival" circuit well, describing such a meeting in his fictional town of Ontarns, where "all of the little river town's saints and sinners were seen nightly, trooping down the one dark street to the town's only church."[73] However, perhaps through marriage or—more probably—through a desire to "get ahead" in business and civic life, he joined the Episcopal Church in Cedar Rapids. The priest at Grace Episcopal, R. J. Campbell, became Sigmund's informal editor on matters religious, which became after 1930 a fairly large task. Sigmund did write verse for Protestant outlets. Typical of these was "Christ in the Street." It describes the crucified Christ returned to a modern city, where he is mocked and abused by the "world—men in the street"; it appeared in *The Christian Century*.[74]

Sigmund's religious passions, though, turned toward the Church of Rome. This began with visits to the Trappist Abbey at New Melleray, on a beautiful hillside southwest of Dubuque, Iowa. Sigmund appears to have written his first poem on the Abbey in the summer of 1930;[75] they would quickly number in the hundreds. He also sent numerous gifts to the monks, including a costly bust of The Sacred Heart in 1934.[76] Sigmund developed a similar relationship with the Dominican Sisters at Saint Clara Convent, just across the Mississippi, on a magnificent bluff near Sinsinawa, Wisconsin. He made several visits to the convent, and gave talks on writing Christian poetry. Sigmund authored over a hundred sonnets about the Sinsinawa nuns, and he shared this verse with them on a regular basis.[77] His verse also appeared in dozens of Catholic periodicals across the country.

These "Catholic" poems are rich in spiritual insight. Some adapt Sigmund's love of nature to religious ends, as in "Choir of the Pines—New Melleray Abbey":

> God tarries here and here He sings;
>   His notes are on the air:
> Some great pines furnish Him the strings
>   For the harp He plays; oh, hallowed things
> These tall trees, marching there!. . . .
>
> And when the abbey's bell-note calls
>   The robed monks to their knees
> There strikes upon the shadowed walk
>   And echoes down the cloistered halls
> These songs from choir-trees.[78]

Sigmund wrote with reverence of The Blessed Virgin; this from a poem to be said before planting time:

Mother of God, we need hillside grass:
    May our beasts fatten here in the stalls,
Ready for April, after storms pass,
    Give us rich harvests through future falls.[79]

Sigmund's reverential treatment of things Catholic extended to the Saints. An example was the sonnet, "A Modernist Speaks to St. Therese":

So close to our own time your span of days
Such little space ago you walked our earth
And knew our era with its hectic ways.
Oh, Little Flower of what unbounded worth
A saint who touched our troubled modern sphere
And saw our present world with all its strife,
This makes it seem you even now are here,
So closely your pure life has brushed our life.

Oh, Flower of Lisieaux, not long ago,
You walked with world folk in your earthly role.
The fragrance of your life stays on I know.
It could not well be otherwise; your soul
in its perfection left us . . . but to those
Who pray to you with faith you still seem close.[80]

Sigmund wrote two dozen poems in which a "World Man" tries to make sense of matters Catholic. Titles included "A World Man Meditates on a Rosary," "A World Man Watches a Priest Celebrate Mass," and "A World Man Meditates on a Statue of Joseph." In one of these, the poet appears to claim his own mystical experience, while sitting in a darkened church before the altar:

Doubter I was but who can make it clear?
Before me stood The Table; seated there,
The Twelve at supper; I was very near
And I take oath that, radiant in His chair
The Master sat; you say it could not be?
Scoff if you must; I plainly saw; 'twas He![81]

A selection of his religious verse appeared in 1931, titled *Altar Panels*.[82]

This intense interest poses the question: Was Jay Sigmund about to convert to Roman Catholicism? The nuns with whom he corresponded certainly thought so. Sister Mary Edmund of the Saint Clara convent told him: "You are spiritually endowed. Let us hope that you will go forward in your search for Truth even as the Wise Men did."[83] After he sent a collection of his "Catholic" sonnets to the Carmelite Nuns in California, the astonished Abbess wrote back: "It is surprising that one not of the Catholic Faith should have so deep an appreciation of things Catholic, especially of the mystical life. Surely you belong to the soul of the Church if you are not one with the body."[84]

My own sense is that Jay Sigmund yearned to make the leap to Rome, but was constrained by the conventions of his time. "Celebrity conversions" to the Catholic faith would not become a phenomenon until the 1940s. Sigmund had already made the great jump from fundamentalist Protestantism to Episcopalianism. His fascination with "things Catholic" might have been tolerated by family, business associates, and friends as another eccentricity in an already somewhat odd man; however, a conversion to Rome in the 1930s could only startle, or shock. Still, perhaps he might have done so after retirement, had not a tragic accident cut his life short.

Bard of the Wapsipinicon

On October 19, 1937, Jay Sigmund went hunting alone near his cottage on the Wapsipinicon River. Hitting a rabbit, he followed the wounded animal up an incline; he slipped and his shotgun discharged, nearly tearing a leg away below the knee. After thirty minutes or so, his shouts attracted the attention of a nearby farmer. The latter summoned a physician and ambulance, but Sigmund "suffered greatly from shock and loss of blood." The next morning, his leg was amputated, but he died an hour later. His funeral, held October 22 at Grace Episcopal Church, drew over 500 mourners; pallbearers included the young Iowan poet Paul Engle and Cedar Rapids "regionalist painter" Marvin Cone.[85]

Eerily, only eleven days before the accident, Sigmund had drafted a "Literary Will," addressed to Paul Engle. "The sudden and unexpected death of two or three friends here of late has made me realize the uncertainty of life," he wrote. He asked Engle to serve as his "literary executor" after his death, "to run over the things I've scribbled off since 1921 and see that any of them worth preserving (if such there be)" were looked after.[86]

In this document, Sigmund offered a remarkably candid and self-effacing assessment of his own work. This should not be a "hard job," he told Engle. "I have written so little of any importance. It may be that there is not a line of any value. Sometimes I think this is true."

Referring to *Frescoes, Pinions,* and *Land O' Maize Folks,* he continued: "[t]he early poems are worthless." Sigmund added: "Possibly everything worthwhile to look over" would be found in *Drowsy Ones, Wapsipinicon Tales, Merged Blood, The Ridge Road, The Least of These,* and the two "Chapbooks" issued by the English Club at Cornell College, *Burroak & Sumac* and *Heron at Sunset.* These were the works that featured more formal verse and focused strictly on the Wapsipinicon Valley. Sigmund also referred briefly to his arrangement with Betty Smith regarding the plays and his unpublished novel, also in her hands. But that was it.[87]

How should we more objectively regard the legacy of Jay Sigmund? Zachary Michael Jack emphasizes his role as a mentor to other Iowa regionalists, including Grant Wood and Paul Engle.[88] Sigmund's influence on Wood was noted earlier. Regarding the latter, Jay Sigmund did "discover" him, so to speak, as a teenager in his Cedar Rapids neighborhood and introduced him to the craft of writing. As Engle's academic career blossomed (his MA thesis won the "Yale Series of Younger Poets" Award in 1931—this was followed by a Rhodes scholarship at Oxford), Sigmund also became his financial advisor. Engle's early collections of verse, especially *Worn Earth* and *Corn,* were solidly regionalist and agrarian in spirit. On Sigmund's death, Engle's comments were generous, and surely genuine:

> I never knew a man who did more good things than Jay Sigmund. I have been helped by him more times than I can remember, and in every possible way. In everything I have written, and all I ever will write, his influence can be traced. He taught me to look at things with honest eyes.[89]

Other contemporaries ably gauged aspects of Sigmund's work. Thomas Cravan, the author and critic who extolled regionalist artists such as Thomas Hart Benton and Grant Wood, encouraged Sigmund in 1935 to write a novel: "[Y]our knowledge of such people exceeds that of, say, Sherwood Anderson, and you have no Freudian theories to propound."[90] Book editor Rousseau Voorhies, an occasional dinner guest at the Sigmund cottage, remarked with insight: "I feel that you are doing with words what Grant Wood is doing with paint."[91] Reviewer Roland White suggested that relative to the global literary scene and over the expanse of a century, "Jay Sigmund was never a *great* writer." And yet, "this not-quite Chekhov of the short story" displayed in both verse and prose qualities described as "genuine," simple, "competent," "authentic," and "alive." Moreover, as Sigmund grew in his understanding of the marginal farmer's plight, he gave "larger place to the human and economic starkness exposed by changing times."[92]

The most accurate appraisal, perhaps, came from a boyhood friend and subsequent small-town newspaper editor, Perry Buxton: "[Jay Sigmund] would take the smoke of autumn fires or the flight of a hawk *and interpret it for us.*"[93]

This *is* the authentic task of any true poet, and—even if such interpretations might convey universal themes—they must always be rooted in the local; as proof, consider Homer's Ithaca.

This is why I suspect that, in the long run, Jay Sigmund will be considered the more important writer than his mentee, Paul Engle. The latter's literary resume is surely much grander. Besides his earlier achievements, Engle would publish another ten collections of verse, several novels and popular remembrances (e.g., the bestselling *An Old-Fashioned Christmas*), select and edit six volumes of *The O'Henry Awards*, win a Pulitzer Prize and an American Book Award, become Poet Laureate of Iowa, serve as director of the famed Iowa Writer's Workshop from 1941 to 1965, and co-found the University of Iowa's International Writing Program. Moreover, technically, Engle's versifying usually did outshine Sigmund's.

When it came to prose, however, Sigmund's sparse, bare, vital short stories are superior to Engle's fictional efforts. More importantly, concerning the regionalist legacy, Jay Sigmund was faithful to his place, to the Wapsipinicon Valley in East-Central Iowa. Even when offered a lucrative business promotion in 1936, he turned it down, because it would mean leaving that valley and moving to Omaha. Paul Engle, in contrast, would chase foreign gods. During the 1940s, his poetry became nationalistic (e.g., *American Child: A Sonnet Sequence*). During the 1960s, he swung fully to the international; indeed, by 1972, he would be co-translator (with his future—and second—wife Hualing Nieh) of the *Poems of Mao Tse-tung*. During the remainder of that decade, he translated poetry collections from Korea, Romania, Japan, Bulgaria, Yugoslavia, Russia, and elsewhere. "Iowa" was lost in this global muddle.

Jay Sigmund, of course, never faced the temptations of post-1940 American jingoism, nor of the "internationalism" which followed. I strongly suspect, though, that if he had, he would have remained content to write poems and stories about his own small place, even if his only audiences were the Scouts at Camp Waubeek and his neighbors and friends. All of his "gods" remained local; his poetic task was to reveal the deeper meanings of everyday events for those among whom he lived. In these senses, he was the better, and the true, Bard of the Wapsipinicon.

Notes

1.   John T. Frederick, "The Younger School," *Palimpest* 11 (February 1930): 80–81; quoted in E. Bradford Burns, *Kinship with the Land: Regionalist Thought in Iowa, 1894–1942* (Iowa City: University of Iowa Press, 1996), 42.
2.   Zachary Michael Jack, *The Plowman Sings: The Essential Fiction, Poetry, and Drama of America's Forgotten Regionalist Jay G. Sigmund* (Lanham, MD: University Press of America, 2008), 14.
3.   Jay G. Sigmund, *Frescoes* (Charleston, SC: Nabu Press, 2011).
4.   "An Announcement of Distinction," *The Cedar Rapids Republican*, [n.d., ca. 1925]; in *Papers of Jay Sigmund (MsC 697)*, Special Collections Department, University of Iowa Libraries [hereafter *Papers*], Box 1, "Newspaper Clippings."
5.   Comments of former neighbor John Wagnor, "Unveil Tablet Honoring Jay Sigmund," newspaper article [n.d.]; *Papers*, Box 1, "Miscellaneous."
6.   Letter, Jay Sigmund to Paul Engle, October 1, 1936; *Papers*, Box 1, File 5.
7.   "An Announcement of Distinction."
8.   Ibid.; "Sigmund, Jay G.—Obituary," *Cedar Rapids Gazette*, October 20, 1937 [typescript]; in *Papers*, Box 1, "Miscellaneous"; and Gaylord Davidson, "Dreamer and Poet Who Does Things in Life Insurance," *The National Underwriter* (August 1924); in *Papers*, Box 4.
9.   "Magazine Writers, Eating Their Way in Tour of Country, Find Mrs. Jay Sigmund An Artist in Her Own Right as a Cook," *Cedar Rapids Gazette* (January 19, 1936): 4; in *Papers*, Box 5.
10.   "Thoughtful, Witty Talk by Author," newspaper article [n.d.]; and "Christopher Morley Impressed by Waubeek 'Enchanting Village,'" *Cedar Rapids Gazette* [n.d.]; both in *Papers*, Box 1, "Newspaper Clippings."
11.   "Obituary," 5.
12.   Zack, *The Plowman Sings*, 5–7.
13.   Ed Ferreter, *Jay Sigmund's Wapsipinicon Valley* (Central City, IA: Pierce Publishing Co., 1987), 27.
14.   Letter, Jay Sigmund to Mrs. Wherry [*Wallaces Farmer*], July 10, 1935; in *Papers*, Box 1, File 5.
15.   "An Announcement of Distinction."
16.   Jay G. Sigmund, *Frescoes* (Boston: B. J. Brimmer Co., 1922), 33.
17.   Sigmund, *Frescoes*, 22–23, 36–38.
18.   "Poetry is for All of Us, Iowa Business—Man Holds," *Mason City Globe-Gazette* (November 20, 1934); in *Papers*, Box 1, "Newspaper Clippings."
19.   Letter, Jay Sigmund to Paul Engle, October 1, 1934; in *Papers*, Box 1, File 5.
20.   Letter, Jay Sigmund to Betty Smith, July 5, 1937; in *Papers*, Box 1, File 7.
21.   Letter, Ruth Suckow to Jay Sigmund, September 4, 1923; in *Papers*, Box 4.

22. Letter, Arthur Davison Ficke to Jay Sigmund, February13, 1937; in *Papers*, Box 1, File 2.

23. "Poetry is For All of Us."

24. Jay G. Sigmund, *Pinions* (New York: James T. White and Co., 1923), 76.

25. Jay G. Sigmund, *Land O'Maize Folks* (New York: James T. White and Co., 1924), 22, 45, 51.

26. Jay G. Sigmund, *Drowsy Ones* (Cedar Rapids, IA: Prairie Publishing Co., 1925), 17–18, 43–45.

27. "A Group of Poems by Jay G. Sigmund," *The Husk* 8 (March 1929): 2.

28. Jay Sigmund, *Burroak & Sumac, Cornell College Chapbook, Number One* (Mt. Vernon, IA: The English Club of Cornell College, n.d.), 23.

29. Letter, Ruth Suckow to Jay Sigmund, September 4, 1923; in *Papers*, Box 4.

30. "An Announcement of Distinction."

31. Burns, *Kinship with the Land*, 46.

32. Charles Finger, "Introduction," in *Wapsipinicon Tales*, ed. Jay G. Sigmund (Cedar Rapids, IA: The Prairie Publishing Company, 1927), 11.

33. Sigmund, *Wapsipinicon Tales*, 25.

34. Jay G. Sigmund, *Merged Blood* (Des Moines, IA: The Maizeland Press, 1929), 73–79, 91–100.

35. Jay G. Sigmund, "Balm," in *The Ridge Road: Short Stories and Poems* (Cedar Rapids, IA: The Prairie Publishing Company, 1930), 36–44.

36. Jay G. Sigmund, "Three Women and a Man," in *The Ridge Road*, 63–67.

37. Letter, Robinson Jeffers to Jay Sigmund, June 22, 1926; in *Papers*, Box 1, File 2.

38. Letter, Lewis Mumford to Jay Sigmund, December 7, 1931; in *Papers*, Box 1, File 1.

39. Letter, Opie Read to Jay Sigmund, June 19, 1927; in *Papers*, Box 1, File 2.

40. Notes, Carl Sandburg to Jay Sigmund, [n.d.]; in *Papers*, Box 4 and Box 1, File 6.

41. "Three of Jay Sigmund's Poems Among Best of Year, Literary Critic Says," newspaper article [n.d.]; in *Papers*, Box 4.

42. Letter, Herbert Redeger to Jay Sigmund, November 16, 1925; in *Papers*, Box 1, File 2.

43. "Current Poetry," *Literary Digest* [n.d., ca. 1926]; in *Papers*, Box 4.

44. Jay Sigmund, "Phantom Horses," in *Burroak & Sumac*, 11; on the award, letter, George Elliston (*Cincinnati Times-Star*) to Jay Sigmund [n.d., ca. 1931]; in *Papers*, Box 1, File 3.

45. "O'Brien Sees Literary Center Shifted from Boston to Iowa," newspaper article [n.d.]; in *Papers*, Box 1, "Newspaper Clippings."

46. Letter, Betty Smith to Jay Sigmund, September 22, 1936; in *Papers*, Box 1, File 6.

47. Sigmund's Three-Act Play "Pitchfork Scepters," the story of a "half Philipino [sic] boy who becomes the Ridge Road Christ," never found a publisher. Sigmund also submitted the draft of a novel to Betty Smith for review. Originally titled *Purple Washboards*, Smith suggested a different title: *Niggerheads*. [!] Fortunately, perhaps, it was never published.

48. Jay Sigmund, "Corn Country Paean," in *Pinions*, 22.

49. Jay G. Sigmund, "Jordan's Grove;" reprinted in Ferreter, *Jay Sigmund's Wapsipinicon Valley*, 5–6.
50. See: Robert L. Dorman, *Revolt of the Provinces: The Regionalist Movement in America, 1920–1945* (Chapel Hill: University of North Carolina Press, 1993), 60, 79–80.
51. Ferreter, *Jay Sigmund's Wapsipinicon Valley*, 2.
52. Jay G. Sigmund, "Anamosa"; reprinted in Ferreter, *Jay Sigmund's Wapsipinicon Valley*, 30–31.
53. Jay G. Sigmund, "Council Rock Song"; reprinted in Ferreter, *Jay Sigmund's Wapsipinicon Valley*, 15.
54. See: Jay G. Sigmund, *The Wapsipinicon: A Poetic Legendary Drama in One Act and Three Scenes*; in *Papers*, Box 2.
55. "To Depict Legend of Wapsie at Camp," newspaper article [n.d.]; in *Papers*, Box 5.
56. "Jay Sigmund's Stories and Poems Are Praised by English Reviewer," newspaper article [n.d., ca. 1931]; in *Papers*, Box 1, "Newspaper Clippings."
57. In "Remarks by Clyde Tull [typescript]," dedication of the Jay Sigmund Park, Waubeek, Iowa, September 27, 1964; in *Papers*, Box 1, Miscellaneous.
58. Letter, Arthur Davison Ficke to Jay Sigmund, June 10, 1937; in *Papers*, Box 1, File 7.
59. Sigmund, *Frescoes*, 30–31.
60. Jay G. Sigmund, *Heron at Sunset. Cornell College Chapbooks: Number Eight* (Mt. Vernon, IA: The English Club of Cornell College, [n.d., ca. 1937-]), 7, 18–19.
61. Jay G. Sigmund, "Tempted"; in *Pinions*, 35.
62. Jay G. Sigmund, "The Younger Ridge Road Men"; in *The Ridge Road*, 75.
63. Jay G. Sigmund, "Bill M' Kellum"; in *Land O' Maize Folks*, 69–70.
64. Jay G. Sigmund, "Retrospect"; in *Land O' Maize Folks*, 87–88.
65. Letter, H. L. Mencken to Jay Sigmund, 20 August [n.d., ca. 1924-]; in *Papers*, Box 4.
66. Jay G. Sigmund, "Meditation;" in *Pinions*, 73.
67. Jay G. Sigmund, "Whistles—Seven A.M.;" in *Pinions*, 79.
68. Jay G. Sigmund, "Corn Country Magnificat"; in *Papers*, Box 2.
69. Jay G. Sigmund, "Christ of the Ridgeroad;" in *Papers*, Box 2.
70. Jay G. Sigmund, "New Master—Old Farm"; in *Heron at Sunset*, 12.
71. Roland A. White, "Book Review of Heron at Sunset," *The Dubuque Leader* (December 24, 1937); in *Papers*, Box 1, "Newspaper Clippings."
72. Jay G. Sigmund, "Asylum Dance"; in *Heron at Sunset*, 18–19.
73. Jay G. Sigmund, "Pleased to Meet You"; in *The Least of These*, 47–53.
74. Jay G. Sigmund, "Christ in the Street"; in *Papers*, Box 2.
75. Letter, Brother Bruno Ryan to Jay Sigmund, August 1, 1930; in *Papers*, Box 1, File 1.
76. Letter, Brother Vincent to Jay Sigmund, December 24, 1934; in *Papers*, Box 1, File 5; and Letter, Brother Bruno to Jay Sigmund, April 11, 1931; in *Papers*, Box 1, File 1.
77. Letter, Sister Mary Samuel to Jay Sigmund, July 28, 1933; in *Papers*, Box 1, File 4.
78. Jay G. Sigmund, "Choir of the Pines—New Melleray Abbey"; in *Papers*, Box 2.

79. Jay G. Sigmund, "Chant for The Blessed Virgin to be Said before Planting Time"; in *Papers*, Box 2.
80. Jay G. Sigmund, "A Modernist Speaks to St. Therese"; in *Papers*, Box 2.
81. Jay G. Sigmund, "A World Man Sees an Altar"; in *Papers*, Box 2.
82. Jay G. Sigmund, *Altar Panels: Twenty Episodes in the Life of Christ* (Milwaukee, WI: Morehouse Publ. Co; London: A. R. Mowbray and Co., 1931).
83. Letter, Sister Mary Edmund to Jay Sigmund, January 8, 1934; in *Papers*, Box 1, File 5.
84. Letter, The Carmelite Nuns to Jay G. Sigmund, March 5, 1936; in *Papers*, Box 1, File 6.
85. "Sigmund, Jay G.—Obituary," 1, 6.
86. Handwritten Document, "To Be Opened At My Death," Jay Sigmund to Paul Engle, October 8, 1937; in *Papers*, Box 1, File 7.
87. "To Be Opened At My Death."
88. Jack, *The Plowman Sings*, 14.
89. "'He Taught Me to Look At Things With Honest Eyes,' says Paul Engle in Writing Poem to Jay Sigmund," *Cedar Rapids Gazette* (October 21, 1937); in *Papers*, Box 1, "Newspaper Clippings."
90. Letter, Thomas Craven to Jay Sigmund, December 20, 1935; in *Papers*, Box 1, File 5.
91. Letter, Rousseau Voorhies to Jay Sigmund, [n.d.]; in *Papers*, Box 1, File 1-B.
92. White, "Review of *Heron at Sunset.*"
93. "Unveil Tablet Honoring Jay Sigmund," newspaper article [n.d.]; in *Papers*, Box 1, "Miscellaneous," (emphasis added).

6

Wilhelm Roepke's Conundrums over the Natural Family

Wilhelm Roepke was an unusual free-market economist working in a difficult time. I believe that we should see him, first of all, as a product of 1914, the year which launched what he called "the devastation on so gigantic a scale to which mankind, then having gone mad, dedicated itself."[1] Mustered to war as a young man, Roepke served in the trenches on the western front. He concluded that a civilization "capable of such monstrous depravity must be thoroughly rotten." Roepke pledged that if he "were to escape from the hell" of the Great War, he would devote his life to "preventing the recurrence of this abomination." He also resolved that war "was simply the rampant essence of the state," collectivism run amuck, and he launched his life long "struggle against economic nationalism . . . monopolies, heavy industry, and large scale farming interests,"[2] all of which he believed had given encouragement to the terrible conflict.

A second starting point for his economic views was Christian. A descendent of German Lutheran pastors, Roepke held to that concept which "makes man the image of God whom it is sinful to use as a means" and who embodies inestimable value as an individual. Noting that the idea of liberty had appeared uniquely in Christian Europe, he concluded "that only a free economy is in accordance with man's [spiritual] freedom and with the political and social structures . . . that safeguard it."[3]

The key pillar of that social structure, Roepke maintained, was the natural family. Along with religion and art, he held that the family did not exist for the state, but was "prestatal, or even suprastatal."[4] In its essence, family life was "natural and free," while the "well ordered house" served as the very foundation of civilization.[5] Derived from "monogam[ous] marriage," the family, he said, was "the original and imperishable basis of every higher community."[6] The "centre of gravity" for planning and living one's life should be in that "most natural of all communities—the family unit."[7] The autonomous family also stood first "in opposition to the arbitrary tendencies of the state."[8] Indeed, the natural family at home became the touchstone of his quest for a truly humane economy.

And yet, despite this strong affirmation of the natural family as critical to free society, Roepke's analysis also led him to several conundrums or dilemmas surrounding family life. For example, he avoided discussing ways in which certain incentives of a free economy might tend to weaken family bonds. Surprisingly, Roepke was also hostile both to the American "Baby Boom" and to the new suburbs in which the young boomers lived. He criticized the creation of large families, although these were in practice a common and fairly natural product of happy home life. For related reasons, he frequently fretted about population growth. Meanwhile, he encouraged public policies that actually had pronatalist, or probirth effects. What were the sources of these conflicting views?

The Humane Economy, Family Style

We should start by examining in more detail *the family nature* of—or the place of the family in—his desired *Humane Economy*. Emerging from the Great War, Roepke found himself engaged in an intellectual battle on two fronts. As he later reported: "I sided with the socialists in their rejection of capitalism, and with the adherents of capitalism in their rejection of socialism."[9] By capitalism, Roepke did not mean the free market. Rather, the term "capitalism" embodied for him "the distorted and soiled form which market economy assumed" in the period between about 1840 and 1940.[10] The liberal quest for economic liberty had gotten off track in this era, he asserted, producing effects that would pave the way for socialist collectivism; specifically:

> . . . the increasing mechanization and prolitarization, the agglomeration and centralization, the growing dominance of the bureaucratic machinery over men, monopolization, the destruction of independent livelihoods . . . and the dissolution of natural ties (the family, the neighborhood, professional solidarity, and others).[11]

The task facing the modern economist, Roepke said, was to eliminate "the sterile alternative" between a return to nineteenth century laissez-faire and twentieth century collectivism. The needed "free economic constitution," as he phrased it, would embrace certain basics: "the market, competition, private initiative, a free price structure, and free choice of consumption."[12] Roepke praised the true market economy as the only system "which releases the full activity of man so natural to him while, at the same time, [curbing] his hidden tigerish tendencies which, unfortunately, are no less natural to him."[13] A system of free economic competition *alone* could deliver "discipline, hard work, decency, harmony, balance, and a just relation between performance and payment."[14] It was also the only system compatible with protection of the free personality, which offered men and women the liberty to tackle challenges in the domains of culture, the intellect, and religion.

All the same, a market economy was not easy to achieve. As Roepke explained, "it is an artistic construction and an edifice of civilization which has this in common with political democracy: it demands and presupposes . . . the most strenuous efforts."[15] Among other needs, the free market required a "high degree of business ethics together with a state ready to protect competition."[16] Looking into the failures of the nineteenth century, Roepke was relentless in exposing the "sins" of monopoly, including:

> Privileges, exploitation . . . the blocking of capital, the concentration of power, industrial feudalism, the restriction of supply and production, the creation of chronic unemployment, the rise in living costs and the widening of social differences, lack of economic discipline, [and] the transformation of industry into an exclusive club, which refuses to accept any new members.[17]

He favored legal devices such as the Sherman Anti-Trust Act found in America to protect competition from these disorders.

Roepke was also an enthusiastic champion of free international commerce. A healthy economy, he insisted, "does not place collectivist shackles on foreign trade." Efforts to build high-tariff walls, he believed, actually "impoverished" small-scale producers. He consistently called for "a liberal and multilateral form of world trade with tolerable tariffs, most-favored-nation clauses, the policy of the open door, the gold standard, and the elimination of closed compulsory [trading] blocks."[18]

The restoration of private property was also central to Roepke's vision. The antithesis to socialist or collectivized man was the property holder. Roepke explained that competition was only one of the pillars of a free economy. The other was personal and familial "self-sufficiency." Accordingly, expansion of the sphere of competition should be balanced by enlarging what he called "the sphere of marketless self-sufficiency." This meant "the restoration of property for the masses," a "lengthy and circumspect" program that would discourage the accumulation of big properties, use "progressive death duties" to break up large estates, and redistribute land to propertyless families on favorable terms. As Roepke wrote: "the industrial worker . . . can and ought to become at least the proprietor of his own residence and garden . . . which would provide him with produce from the land." This alone would render each family "independent of the tricks of the market with its wage and price complexities and its business fluctuations."[19]

Indeed, Roepke held an almost religious faith in the transformative power of the private garden. As he wrote, the keeping of a family garden "was not only 'the purest of human pleasures' but also offers the indispensable *natural foundation* for family life and the upbringing of children." In praising the "Magnetism of the Garden,"[20] he told the story of a friend who was showing the family gardens of several workers to a "dogmatic old-time liberal"; some think this was Ludwig von Mises. In any case, Roepke continued: "on seeing these happy people spending their free evenings in their gardens," the laissez-faire liberal "could think of nothing better than the cool remark this was an *irrational* form of vegetable production." Roepke retorted: "He could not get it into his head that it was a very rational form of 'happiness production' which surely is what matters most."[21]

Still, Roepke acknowledged that it was not certain "that people really want to possess property." Actually, "to hold" land presupposed much more: "frugality, the capacity to weigh up the present and the future, a sense of continuity and preservation, the will to independence, [and] an outstanding family feeling."[22]

The necessary task, he said, was broader still: a "deproletarization" that would take industrial workers who lacked roots in "home, property, environment, family, and occupation" and transform them into free men. This meant, in Roepke's mind, "rendering the working and living conditions of the industrial worker as similar to the positive aspects of the life of the peasant as possible." Beyond his praise for family garden homes, the economist celebrated businesses like Switzerland's Bally Shoe Company which actively assisted its workers in acquiring houses and land, and supported their small agricultural endeavors with ploughing services, fertilizers, locally adapted seeds, and special animal stock. All of these initiatives were designed, Roepke said, "to save [these families] from their proletarian existence."[23]

To heal the distortions of human life wrought by nineteenth century laissez-faire capitalism, Roepke even sought to undo—in some degree—the urban-industrial revolution. Writing in *The Social Crisis of Our Time*, he called for nothing less than the "drastic decentralization of cities and industries, [and] the restoration of some more 'natural order.'"[24] He labeled the modern big city a "monstrous abnormality," a "pathological degeneracy" that devitalized human existence, adding: "the pulling down of this product of modern civilization is one of the most important aims of social reform."[25] Relative to the decentralization of industry, he urged that "the artisan and the small trader" receive "all the well-planned assistance that is possible." He also saw promise in the rise of the "tertiary," or service sector. Moreover, Roepke believed that recent technological advances—electric motors, the internal combustion engine, compact machine tools—lent new competitive advantages to small enterprises. Anticipating *Prairie Home Companion*'s Garrison Keillor (who has said that you buy local products at Ralph's Pretty Good Grocery in Lake Wobegon instead of at the Mall in St. Cloud, because Ralph is your neighbor), Roepke urged that consumers "should not shrink from the sacrifice of a few cents in order to carry out an economic policy of their own and support [local] artisans to the best of their ability and for the good of the community."[26]

This process of "deproletarization" also meant restoration of a peasantry: a countryside of small family farms. Roepke called the peasantry "the very cornerstone of every healthy social structure" and "the backbone of a healthy nation." He continued: "A peasant who is unburdened by debt and has an adequate holding is the freest and most independent man among us." The peasant household also showed "that a type of family is possible which gives each member a productive function and thus becomes *a community for life*, solving all problems of education and age groups in a natural manner." Given these qualities, Roepke held that "a particularly high degree of farsighted, protective, directive, regulating, and balancing intervention [by the state in agriculture] is not only defensible, but even mandatory." He looked with particular admiration to the relatively advanced peasant farming systems then found in Switzerland, Scandinavia, Holland, Belgium, and France, and he looked with particular hope to the prospects for specialized production in dairy, eggs, meats, fruits, and vegetables.[27]

Another component of the humane economy would be a limited, but real welfare or social security system. Roepke did condemn the cradle-to-grave approach of Great Britain and Scandinavia, where "a large part of private income is continually being fed into the pumping station of the welfare state and redistributed by the state, with considerable wastage in the process." He stressed the corrupting effects on the broader economy of this "everything in one pot, everything out of one pot" scheme, including the suppression of capital investment, the loss of individual initiative, and inflation.[28] Moreover, such a system was like "a powerful machine that has neither brakes nor reverse gear,"[29] ever encroaching "upon the area of self-providence and mutual aid" so that "the capacity [and willingness] to provide for oneself and for members of one's family . . . diminishes."

All the same, Roepke acknowledged the need for "a certain minimum of compulsory state institutions for social security." There must "naturally be room," he said, for public old-age pensions, health and accident insurance, widow's benefits, and unemployment relief in a "sound . . . system in a free society." The imperative was to keep the scheme limited, providing only a floor of support. He had special praise for the Swiss and American Social Security systems, circa 1960, which recognized and defended these necessary limits.[30]

Roepke called his whole program a "Third Way," one which would reconcile "the immense advantages of the free market economy with the claims of social justice, stability, dispersal of power, [and] fairness."[31] This program favored "the ownership of small- and medium-sized properties, independent farming, the decentralization of industrial areas, the restoration of the dignity and meaning of work, the reanimation of professional pride and . . . ethics, [and] the promotion of community solidarity."[32] This Third Way also sought "the organic building-up of society from natural and neighborly communities . . . starting with the family through parish and county to nation." Alone, this Third Way rendered "possible a healthy family life and a non-artificial manner of bringing up children."[33] Indeed, "simple, natural happiness" would come from placing humans "in the true community that begins in the family" and exists "in harmony with nature."[34]

The Costs of Family Decay

Viewing the Western world in the middle decades of the twentieth century, Roepke identified the negative consequences of "spiritual collectivism, proletarization . . . and centralization," the "most serious" of which was "the disintegration of the family." Usually propertyless and without productive function, the modern family was "degraded to a mere consumers cooperative . . . often without children . . . or without the possibility of bestowing on them more than a summary education."[35] Along with this "disruption of the Family" went "the loss of a sense of 'generations' [where] the individual loses . . . his sense of the continuity of time and the relationship of the dead to the living and [of] the living to their successors."[36] Things were "fundamentally wrong," Roepke said, in those nations "where the most natural actions of man like . . . caring for his family, saving, creating new things or raising children must be instigated by propaganda . . . [or] moralizing."[37]

And yet, Roepke's analysis of and prescription for the social crisis of his age involved troubling paradoxes or dilemmas over the natural family. For example, where his contemporary Joseph Schumpeter and later analysts, such as Daniel Bell, argued that certain incentives within the market economy tended to weaken family bonds,[38] Roepke seemed unconcerned. Notably, he largely ignored the market's latent demand for the labor of married women. He did argue that family was "the natural sphere of the woman" and that the decay of autonomous homes made "the female half of society" into real victims, but he apparently did not see this in any way as the result of legitimate market incentives. Instead, Roepke seemed to blame the "bad" capitalism of the nineteenth century for this result.[39]

It was true, of course, that equity feminism—a common companion to a free labor market—had made little headway into his model domain of mid-twentieth century Switzerland. Most married women there were still *hausfrauen*, or housewives; indeed, women did not even gain the vote in that Alpine land until 1971, five years after his death. Roepke simply assumed that the male breadwinner/female homemaker family would prevail in the humane economy.

Roepke was also direct witness to the burgeoning American suburbs of the 1940s and 1950s, where young adults fled the overcrowded cities to create child-centered homes, each complete with housewife, lawn, and garden. And yet, instead of praising this process as an aspect of decentralization, he condemned these new creations. At the more objective level, he pointed to "the danger that [such] decentralization will become a mere extension of the big city into the country along the main roads." This would amount "to a mere decentralization of sleeping quarters whereas the big city would still remain the center of work, shopping and pleasure."[40] Meanwhile, he predicted that traffic problems derived from suburbia would grow insoluble, creating a "hell of congestion."

At a more viscereal level, Roepke objected to the superficial charm and hyper-"gregariousness" of the new American suburbs. "Everybody is forever 'dropping in' on everybody else," he complained. "The agglomeration of people [in the suburb] stifles all expression of individuality, any attempt at keeping to oneself; every aspect of life is centrally ruled." Roepke especially indicted the "pressure . . . to take part in [suburban] communal life . . . unless [one] wants to be known as a spoilsport." He concluded that trying "to escape from the giant honeycombs of city dwelling, into the suburbs is to jump from the frying pan into the fire."[41]

More curiously, this great champion of the "natural family" showed an emotional dislike of human numbers, involving direct and implied condemnation of the large family. In *A Humane Economy*, for example, Roepke complained about "the visible crowdedness of our existence, which seems to get irresistibly worse every day," the "masses of people who are all more or less the same," the "overwhelming quantities of man-made things everywhere, the traces of people," "this deluge of sheer human quantity," and the emergence of humankind as the "parasite of the soil."[42]

Roepke did recognize on occasion the reality of antinatalist tendencies in modern life. In his 1932 work, *What's Wrong With the World?*, he linked the global agricultural depression of the prior decade to "the slowing up of the growth in population."[43] He acknowledged that birth control "techniques which permit the separation of sexuality and procreation" spread ever more widely. He continued: "Old mores have succumbed to new attitudes until the practice of birth control has become increasingly a simple matter of habit." Roepke attributed the use of birth control, in part, to "deliberate selfishness" and concluded that "the modern rationalist spirit" could "drag down both the birth rate and the moral health of the nation." He even acknowledged that "the birth rate . . . can theoretically fall to zero . . . resulting in an absolute diminution of population."[44]

However, his more usual message was a condemnation of those economists who defended population growth as a good. Roepke denounced the "blindness," the "criminal optimism," and the "strange mixture of statistics and lullabies" which overlooked the dangers of expanding human numbers. He denied the "bold theory" that it was population growth "which imparts dynamism to the industrial counties." He mocked the argument that "the more cradles there are in use, the greater is the demand for goods, the higher is the invest-ment . . . the more vigorous is the boom." He labeled it "a degradation of man and of the great mystery of creation to turn conception and birth" into vehicles for economic expansion. Roepke considered the formation of a large family to be an *ir*responsible act. He pointed to the baby boom in America, fueled by an average family size of about four children, as particularly "new and disturbing."[45] He concluded: "Every thinking person must . . . admit that, sooner or later, it will become necessary to restrain such population increases. . . . So why not sooner than later?"[46]

How might we explain these views? To begin with, Roepke advanced the argument that the processes of industrialization, centralization, and proletarization were in fact the *consequence* of too many children. During the nineteenth century, he explained, birth rates in Europe had remained high while death rates fell, producing "the swamping effect of the incredible increase of population." Roepke noted that each new generation is like a horde of little barbarians. If parents could not tame them, disaster resulted, adding:

> Now since this increase in population took place largely in cir-cumstances and among classes in which this taming, i.e., cultural assimilation was less and less successful, we have been obliged in effect to experience a barbarian invasion out of the lap of our own nation.[47]

This flooding of the earth with a "mass" was "bound to stamp its mass character" on the whole civilization. It had produced an "orgy of technology," "mammoth industries," "bloated big cities," a "materialist and rationalist life without tradition," "the undermining of everything permanent and rooted," and "the subjugation of the whole globe by a mechanical, positivist civilization." Roepke asserted that it would be impossible to build a humane economy "when the industrial nations of the West are improvidently taking a new demographic upsurge for granted."[48]

Second, he embraced an analytical Malthusianism premised on the calculation of an optimum population for each nation. While the Reverend T. R. Malthus had failed as an immediate prophet, Roepke said, the Anglican priest had correctly asked why every economic gain achieved by "the labors and ingenuity of the existing population" should be immediately "claimed by millions of new individuals instead of serving to increase the well-being of those now on earth."[49]

And third, like many other mid-century analysts, Roepke grew mesmerized by population growth projections which counted 300 billion inhabitants on the earth by the year 2300. In such an anthill existence, he asked, what would happen to those "unbought graces of life": "nature, privacy, beauty, dignity, birds and woods and fields and flowers, repose and true leisure."[50]

Roepke insisted that "a stabilization of population" was "an indispensable prerequisite of the restoration to health of our society." Yet he was vague in explaining how to reach this goal. In one passage, he suggested that the three-child family would allow for "a healthy and normal family life" while "in no way" opposing "the stabilization of population."[51] In another place, though, he implied that "overpopulation" in Europe would require a two-child or even one-child family system to restore economic equilibrium.[52]

In retrospect, we can see that Roepke greatly overestimated the procreative potential of late twentieth century Western peoples. The surge in numbers during the nineteenth century was over by 1920. Indeed, fertility had been falling throughout Europe, North America, and Australia–New Zealand since at least 1880; and in France and the United States, since 1820. Post–World War II "baby booms" were fragile events, the products of unique social forces that would not last. Postfamily attitudes, closely linked to a strange combination of democratic socialism with secular individualism, eventually carried the day. As would be clear by the year 2000, below-replacement fertility and depopulation represented the real Western future.[53]

In his public advocacy, Roepke posed still other dilemmas regarding the natural family. For example, his plan to resettle industrial families in semirural homes, complete with a vegetable garden and simple animal husbandry, ran counter to his demographic goals. As he was well aware, such an existence would give "the family with many children those conditions which transform a heavy burden to be endured . . . into something natural, stimulating and immediately worthwhile."[54] As an economist, Roepke should have realized that this would in turn create incentives for more children, for larger families. Put another way, his goal of fertility limitation would have been best achieved by leaving families in large cities where children became ever more costly luxuries.

A similar contradiction emerged in his advocacy regarding social security. As noted earlier, Roepke urged creation of a limited system of public pensions, "putting a floor" under the feet of "the weak and helpless" and preventing their fall "into bitter distress and poverty; no less, *no more.*" Such a system, he insisted, should not drive out other forms of old-age support, including private savings and annuities and the aid provided to aging parents by grown children.[55]

Roepke was *right* in seeing such a system as possible and socially constructive. Ironically, though, new research shows that moderate-sized public pensions such as those found in the United States during the 1950s actually have *a positive effect* on fertility: that is, they encourage larger families. Indeed, it appears that the pre-1965 American system of limited state pensions was a contributing factor to the baby boom.[56]

Conversely, it has been fairly clear since the late 1930s that large, publicly funded pensions *discourage* fertility and larger families. Explained briefly, such a system socializes the "insurance value" of children, thus, punishing parents who raise the young while rewarding their "free riding," childless neighbors.[57] Once again, if a decline in fertility was his primary goal, Roepke should have encouraged ever larger state pensions.

Roepke as Successful Prophet

Fortunately, though, Roepke's priority lay elsewhere. While raising the matter in the context of the population question, he had a larger purpose in asking:

> [W]hat happens to man and his soul? What happens to the things which cannot be produced or expressed in monetary terms . . . but which are the ultimate conditions of man's happiness and of the fullness and dignity of his life?[58]

In finding answers, Roepke was—and is—correct in trying to rehabilitate social life by returning human beings to decentralized, autonomous, self-sufficient, functional homes, where education and real work would be reintegrated into the daily flow of family living. Toward this end, he correctly saw mid-twentieth century Switzerland to be a model state. "As the common enterprise of freedom-loving peasants and burghers," he wrote, "it has offered the world a living example of the harmonious integration of [rural] and city culture."[59] He described a real village of about 3,000 people with nearby farmsteads in the Bern-Mittelland, a place which combined artisan shops, small factories, a brewery, a dairy for cheese, a "highly tasteful" book store, and "a great collection of obviously thriving crafts and craftsmen." He added "that the whole place is remarkable for its cleanliness and sense of beauty; its inhabitants dwell in houses which anyone might envy; each garden is lovingly and expertly tended; [and] antiquity is protected. . . . *This village is our ideal* translated into a highly concrete reality."[60]

Roepke's analysis also points toward ways to achieve this ideal in our new century.

- His goal of "genuine decentralization" through "the creation of fresh small centers in lieu of the big city" anticipates the New Urbanism of our day, where attention to the physical settings of real neighborhoods combines with a reattachment of work and retail sites to family residences.[61]
- Roepke's reminder that certain technological innovations may support the broad dispersal of productive work gains new importance in the age of the home computer and the extraordinary economic democracy of the Internet. Indeed, the German-Swiss economist had challenged technologists "to serve decentralization instead of centralization, rendering possible the greatest possible number of independent existences and giving back to human beings as producers and workers a state of affairs which would make them happy and satisfy their more elementary and most legitimate instincts."[62]
- Roepke's attention to "tertiary production," or the service sector, as a growing sphere for human labor again enhances the prospects for small and medium businesses which might support household independence.[63]
- And Roepke's insights regarding the competitive advantages held by small-family farms in the production of specialty crops gains new relevance in the age of organics.[64]

These are the areas where Roepke succeeded as both analyst and prophet. He was also prophetic in seeing that the civilizational crisis of the Christian West deriving from "a cultural retreat . . . a squandering of our inheritance" was linked to "a continuous process of secularization."[65] He wrote that the core of "the malady from which our civilization suffers lies in the individual soul," adding that this disease would also only be "overcome within the individual soul."[66] Here, too, we can safely conclude that Roepke was altogether correct.

Notes

1. Wilhelm Roepke, *What's Wrong with the World?* (Philadelphia: Dorrance & Company, 1932), 21.

2.   Wilhelm Roepke, "The Economic Necessity of Freedom," *Modern Age* 3 (Summer 1959): 228–31.
3.   Roepke, "The Economic Necessity of Freedom," 233.
4.   Wilhelm Roepke, "The Place of the Nation," *Modern Age* 10 (Spring 1966): 129.
5.   Wilhelm Roepke, *A Humane Economy: The Social Framework of the Free Market* (Wilmington, DE: ISI Books, 1998), 40, 177. [Hereafter, *Humane Economy*]
6.   Wilhelm Roepke, *The Moral Foundations of Civil Society* (New Brunswick, NJ: Transaction Publishers, 1996), 133. [Hereafter, *Moral Foundations*]
7.   Wilhelm Roepke, *Welfare, Freedom and Inflation* (Birmingham: University of Alabama Press, 1964), 42.
8.   Roepke, *Moral Foundations*, 110–11.
9.   Roepke, "The Economic Necessity of Freedom," 231.
10. Roepke, *Moral Foundations*, 27.
11. Wilhelm Roepke, *The Social Crisis of Our Time* (New Brunswick, NJ: Transaction Publishers, 1992), 176. [Hereafter, *Social Crisis*]
12. Roepke, *Moral Foundations*, 32.
13. Wilhelm Roepke, *The Problem of Economic Order* (Cairo: National Bank of Egypt, 1951), 13.
14. Roepke, *Social Crisis*, 182.
15. Roepke, *Moral Foundations*, 28.
16. Roepke, *Social Crisis*, 227–28.
17. Ibid., 229–30.
18. Ibid., 209, 242.
19. Roepke, *Moral Foundations*, 159.
20. Ibid., 159–60.
21. Roepke, *Social Crisis*, 224.
22. Roepke, *Moral Foundations*, 156.
23. Roepke, *Social Crisis*, 221, 226.
24. Ibid., 235.
25. Roepke, *Moral Foundations*, 161–62.
26. Roepke, *Social Crisis*, 214–17.
27. Roepke, *Social Crisis*, 201–16.
28. Roepke, *Welfare, Freedom and Inflation*, 37–41.
29. Wilhelm Roepke, *Against the Tide* (Chicago, IL: Henry Regnery Company, 1969), 205.
30. Roepke, *Humane Economy*, 175–80.
31. Roepke, *The Problem of Economic Order*, 38.
32. Wilhelm Roepke, *Economics of the Free Society* (Chicago, IL: Henry Regnery Company, 1963), 257.
33. Roepke, *Moral Foundations*, 154
34. Roepke, "The Economic Necessity of Freedom," 235.
35. Roepke, *Social Crisis*, 15, 32.
36. Roepke, *Moral Foundations*, 134–35.
37. Roepke, *The Problem of Economic Order*, 13.
38. See: Joseph Schumpeter, *Capitalism, Socialism and Democracy* (New York: Harker and Brothers 1962 [1942]); and Daniel Bell, *The Cultural Contradictions of Capitalism* (New York: Basic Books, 1976).

39. Roepke, *Social Crisis*, 15–16.
40. Roepke, *Moral Foundations*, 162.
41. Roepke, *Humane Economy*, 40.
42. Ibid., 39, 42, 44.
43. Roepke, *What's Wrong With the World?*, 24.
44. Roepke, *Economics of the Free Society*, 55.
45. Roepke, *Humane Economy*, 42–48.
46. Roepke, *Economics of the Free Society*, 62.
47. Roepke, *Moral Foundations*, 135–36.
48. Roepke, *Social Crisis*, 13; Roepke, *Humane Economy*, 45–46.
49. Roepke, *Economics of the Free Society*, 56–60.
50. Roepke, *Humane Economy*, 44, 49.
51. Roepke, *Moral Foundations*, 136.
52. Roepke, *Humane Economy*, 49.
53. See: Allan Carlson, *Fractured Generations* (New Brunswick, NJ: Transaction Publishers, 2005), 15–34.
54. Roepke, *Moral Foundations*, 159–60.
55. Roepke, *Welfare, Freedom and Inflation*, 24–25.
56. Berthold U. Wigger, "Pay-As-You-Go Financed Public Pensions in A Model of Endogenous Growth and Fertility," *Journal of Population Economics* 12 (1999): 625.
57. See: Gunnar Myrdal, *Population: A Problem for Democracy* (Cambridge, MA: Harvard University Press, 1940): 197–200; Charles F. Hohm, et al., "A Reappraisal of the Social Security-Fertility Hypotheses: A Bidirectional Approach," *The Social Science Journal* 23 (1986): 163; and Isaac Ehrlich and Francis T. Liu, "Social Security, the Family, and Economic Growth," *Economic Inquiry* 36 (July 1998): 404.
58. Roepke, *Humane Economy*, 48.
59. Roepke, *Social Crisis*, 25.
60. Roepke, *Moral Foundations*, 31.
61. Ibid., 163.
62. Ibid., 173, 178.
63. Ibid., 176.
64. Lynn Miller, "Inside the Circle," *Small Farmers' Journal* 31 (Summer 2007): 5.
65. Roepke, *Social Crisis*, 7.
66. Roepke, "The Economic Necessity of Freedom," 236.

7

Russell Kirk: Northern Agrarian

In his autobiographical *The Sword of Imagination*, conservative man-of-letters Russell Kirk labels himself "a Northern Agrarian."[1] The same label surfaces in *American Conservatism: An Encyclopedia*, where the editors place poet Robert Frost and the Democratic politician Eugene McCarthy alongside Kirk as Northern Agrarians.[2] What is meant by this curious term?

A possible answer would be to reference the great Northern Agrarian of a century ago, Liberty Hyde Bailey. In that era, farming news was still national news, and Professor Bailey—largely forgotten today—was then a celebrity of near rock-star proportions. Like Kirk, Bailey was born in a village in western Michigan: albeit sixty years earlier. Also like Kirk, Bailey graduated from the Michigan State College of Agriculture in East Lansing, and later returned to teach there. Bailey went on to assume—in 1888—the chair of Practical and Experimental Horticulture at Cornell University. He was the founding editor of the journals *Country Life in America* and the *Cornell Countryman*. In 1904, Bailey founded the pathbreaking College of Agriculture at Cornell, becoming its first dean. Four years later, President Theodore Roosevelt appointed Bailey as Chairman of the National Commission on Country Life. Its 1909 report called for rebuilding a great agricultural civilization in America. Bailey's important agrarian books included *The Outlook to Nature*, *The Holy Earth*, and *The Country-Life Movement in the United States*.

Was Kirk in the mold of Bailey? There are similarities. For example, they shared a love of the garden and the forest. Dean Bailey had a lifelong interest in raspberries, blackberries, and other brambles by the woods, and authored several massive volumes on this genus. At his upstate New York home, he maintained a large garden, including a portion devoted to weeds, studying and praising these usually despised plants for their role in renewing damaged soil. Kirk, too, relished the time he devoted to the care of his five acres in Mecosta, Michigan. He loved his garden and planted hundreds of trees on his family land and in the village. As daughter Andrea recalls:

> Agrarian life was well understood and appreciated by my father. Under the dimming September sun he and I worked together planting and pruning. He loved to watch the progress his labors had achieved; the growth of new life from his ancestral earth.[3]

Bailey and Kirk also shared a sympathy for Thomas Jefferson's vision of agrarian democracy. For Bailey, the farmer remained "the fundamental fact in democracy" because he had been granted "the keepership of the earth." Farmers formed "a natural correction against organization men, habitual reformers, and extremists."[4] For his part, Kirk also declared early on his admiration for the free rural yeomanry. As he wrote in his first published essay, appearing in 1941:

> To plan effectively the nation's future we must foster Jeffersonian principles. We must have slow but democratic decisions, sound local government, diffusion of property-owning, taxation as direct as possible, preservation of civil liberties, payment of debts by the generation incurring them . . . a stable and extensive agriculture . . . and, above all, stimulation of self-reliance.[5]

He added: "Jeffersonianism may die, but, stand or fall, it has made manifest its essential rightness and its essential virtue."[6]

And yet, there were large differences between the two. Bailey's northern agrarianism was rooted in the sciences, in botany, horticulture, and ecology. Kirk's agrarian vision rested instead on history, biography, and literature. Bailey was a great believer in agricultural education and in the extension service, which would bring plant and animal sciences from the universities into the countryside. Kirk held Michigan State College and other land-grant agricultural schools largely in contempt, dismissing them as "cow colleges." Bailey was an activist and progressive, seeking to "uplift" the farm population into a new civilization. Kirk was a conservative, distrusting novelty. "Change is not reform," he learned from the past. Kirk wanted to save and protect farm families, not "uplift" them.

Indeed, Kirk's real sympathies lay with a different sort of agrarianism, the southern kind. He seems to have discovered the Southern Agrarians in 1938. When browsing through the Michigan State bookstore, he found poet and essayist Donald Davidson's new volume, *The Attack on Leviathan: Regionalism and Nationalism in the United States.* Kirk reported later: "It was written eloquently, and for me it made coherent the misgivings I had felt concerning the political notions popular in the 1930s. The book was so good that I assumed all intelligent Americans . . . were reading it."[7] In fact, Kirk later learned that the publisher—the University of North Carolina Press—had pulped most of the printed copies after distributing but a few hundred.

Davidson's influence on him grew. Kirk became fond of the Southerner's poetry. Kirk quoted frequently from one of Davidson's anticity poems, "The Long Street":

> The grass cannot remember; trees cannot
> Remember what once was here . . .
> And the baked curve of asphalt, smooth trodden
> Covers dead earth that once was quick with grass.
> Snuffing the ground with acrid breath the motors
> Fret the long street. Steel answers steel. Dust whirls.
> Skulls hurry past with the pale flesh yet clinging
> And a little hair.

Kirk himself also read the Twelve Southerners' great 1930 Manifesto, *I'll Take My Stand*, a volume informally edited by Davidson. Here Kirk found:

> Christian humanism, stern criticism of the industrialized mass society, detestation of communism and other forms of collectivism, attachment to the ways of the Old South—such were the principles uniting the Southern Agrarians.[8]

Kirk himself moved south in 1940, earning a master's degree at Duke University. He wrote his thesis on John Randolph of Roanoke, the early American statesman who believed that "the agricultural life is the best state of society man can ask." As Kirk explained, Randolph "declared the real substance of society to be the independent planters and farmers of small freeholds." Judging Old Republicans like Randolph, Kirk concluded: "in many ways the life they sought to perpetuate was good."[9]

Kirk also befriended Richard Weaver, the southern-born professor of English at the University of Chicago and author, most famously, of *Ideas Have Consequences*. While "a declared Southerner," as Kirk put it, Weaver was somewhat unusual in his admiration for Abraham Lincoln, a legacy of the pro-Union Mountain Whigs of eastern Tennessee. All the same, both Weaver and Kirk—in the latter's words—"were defenders of immemorial ways, old morals, old customs, old loves, the wisdom of the species, the life of rural regions, and little communities."[10]

Another attachment by Kirk to the southern way came through his fondness for the work of Orestes Brownson. Kirk saw this Yankee convert to Roman Catholicism as "the most interesting example of the progress of Catholicism as a conservative spirit in America."[11] The Texan M. E. Bradford once labeled Brownson as Kirk's "neglected predecessor in American thought," particularly as a northern defender of the southern people and way-of-life.[12] Indeed, Kirk often lamented "the disappearance of [the] Southern architectural style" and of "the sort of schooling" that had produced men like Davidson and his brother agrarians. Kirk concluded:

> Southern agrarians proclaimed when I was a child that the southern culture is worth defending; that society is something more than the Gross National Product; that the country lane is healthier than the Long Street; that more wisdom lies in Tradition than in Scientism; that Leviathan is a devourer, not a savior.[13]

Surely, it is no coincidence that a majority of Kirk's "canons of conservatism" are distinctly "Southern Agrarian" in tone, notably:

- "Affection for the proliferating variety and mystery of human existence . . .";
- "Conviction that civilized society requires orders and classes . . .";
- "Tradition and sound prejudice provide checks upon man's anarchic impulse . . ."; and
- "Innovation is a devouring conflagration more often than it is a torch of progress."

However, a better way to understand Kirk as a Northern Agrarian may be through other, and in some ways, more primordial themes that run through his work: themes that reveal the hard edge of Kirk's defense of the permanent things.

First, Disdain for the Modern City. Kirk noted Randolph's "detestation of towns."[14] Kirk focused his own ire on ugly urban sprawl, the desecration of landscape and soil by suburbs and malls. As he wrote in his textbook on *Economics*: "some of the best soil in the United States has disappeared before urban sprawl or has been covered by great highways."[15] Referring to Long Island, he wrote:

During the late fifties and early sixties, I watched . . . the devastation
of what had been a charming countryside, as dismaying as what was
being done to our cities. To make room for a spreading population was
necessary: but to do it hideously and stupidly was not ineluctable.[16]

Looking closer to home, Kirk remarked: "This brutal destruction . . .
of the very landscape, in this age of the bulldozer, constitutes a bel-
ligerent repudiation of what we call tradition. It is a rejection of our
civilized past."[17]

Second, Wariness Toward Industrial Civilization. John Crowe Ransom, one of the Twelve Southerners, called industrialism a force "of
almost miraculous cunning but no intelligence."[18] Kirk, too, wrote of
"the collective cunning" possessed by "industrial forces."[19] In 1941,
he held a job at Ford Motor Company's mammoth Rouge plant:
"a fearful and wonderful sight," Kirk called it, a place which made him
"shiver."[20] He wrote of the Industrial Revolution as a powerful foe: it
"turned the world inside out. Personal loyalties gave way to financial
relationships. . . . Industrialism was a harder knock to conservatism
than the books of the French equalitarians."[21] Kirk blasted the Austrian
neoliberal economists for not seeing "the ugliness, the monotony, the
ennui of modern industrial existence"; he labeled the factory city of
Flint, Michigan, as "one of the most grim and hideous towns in the
whole world."[22] He saw "modern industrial production . . . using up
forests, fossil fuels, mineral deposits, and other natural resources at
an alarming rate."[23] Writing in 1991, he despaired over "the industrial
unification" of the earth, explaining:

> . . . nowadays the whole of the world must be subjected to those
> environmental mischiefs and social discontents that already have
> worked immense harm in the 'developed countries.'[24]

Third, A Suspicion of Raw Capitalism. The contemporary agrarian
writer Wendell Berry labels capitalism "the economy of the bulldozer"[25];
the Twelve Southerners called modern advertising "the great effort of
a false economy of life to approve itself."[26] Kirk was always careful to
affirm his admiration for economic liberty, terming "free enterprise . . .
the most productive and most liberal economic arrangement con-
ceivable." However, he faulted libertarian economists such as Ludwig
von Mises and Friedrich Hayek for the narrowness of their economic
thought. "American conservatives," Kirk declared, "ought to talk a good
deal less about the laws of economics and a great deal more about the

laws of justice." He noted that von Mises dismissed traditionalism as hostile to scientific truth and then lamented the success of anticapitalist propaganda. Kirk responded:

> This bold economist seems willfully oblivious to the historical truth that men respect property, private rights, and order in society out of deference to the 'myths' von Mises tries to dissipate, the 'myths' of divine social intent, of tradition, of natural law.

Pointing again to the Austrian neoliberals, Kirk continued:

> Theirs is a doctrine which destroys itself in proportion as it is generally promulgated: once supernatural and traditional sanctions are dissolved, economic self-interest is ridiculously inadequate to hold an economic system together, and even less adequate to preserve order.[27]

Put another way, the market economy could only survive within a matrix of custom, religion, and community. Kirk agreed with economic historian Karl Polanyi that the laissez-faire system was not a natural product of history; rather, it "was brought into existence" as a companion to the centralizing state. He also praised sociologist Robert Nisbet's call for a new kind of laissez-faire, "in which the basic unit" would *not* be the individual, but rather "the social group": "church, family, guild or union, local community, school and university."[28]

Fourth, A Respect for the Vital, Function-Rich Family. Kirk favorably quoted Randolph on the superiority of the rural, or yeoman farm baby compared to both its urban or aristocratic counterpart:

> The rickety and scrafulous little wretch who first sees light in a workhouse, or in a brothel and who feels the effects of alcohol before the effects of vital air, is not equal in any respect to the ruddy offspring of the honest yeoman; nay, I will go further, and say that a prince, provided he is no better born than royal blood will make him, is not equal to the healthy son of a peasant.[29]

Kirk attributed this advantage held by rural children to the function-rich nature of their homes. In an age largely celebrating the "companionship family" resting on psychological nuances, Kirk yearned for a hardier model. The skills of husbandry and housewifery; the varied tasks of the farmer and the farm wife; the foundation of children's moral and practical education in their homes[30]: these were the sources of healthy, happy, and hopeful children. In economist Wilhelm Röpke's work, Kirk found a "Third Way" economic humanism that would restore "property, function, and dignity to the mass of men." According to Kirk, those seeking a viable future "will endeavor to make the family function as a device for love and education and economic *advantage*, not simply an instrument of the feeding-and-housing-and-procreative process."[31]

Fifth, A Regard for Economic Independence. The agrarian novelist Louis Bromfield praised the "old economic independence of the farmer, his sense of security, that stability which a healthy agriculture gives to the economy of any nation."[32] While certainly not a farmer, Kirk personally aspired to the same end. As Bruce Frohnen remarks, Kirk wished to lead "a life of 'decent independence.'" He sought "to provide for his family . . . free from compromising entanglements" and "without fear of the taxman, the bank repossessor, or an angry patron."[33] He became an independent scholar, an author and lecturer dependent only on his wit and skills. Kirk hoped that all persons would enjoy the same autonomy. He urged that they try "to make their profession, or trade, or craft an instrument not merely for private profit, but for satisfying their own desire to feel that somehow they matter." To "deproletarianize" industrial workers, Kirk had his own prescription: create "[f]amily farms, family cooperation, . . . the diminution of the average size of factories, the gradual substitution for 'the old-style welfare policy' of an intelligent trend toward self-sufficiency." He favorably quoted Röpke, who contrasted, at one end, the American cash-crop farmer who bought his food in a supermarket with "[a]t the other, more fortunate end . . . the industrial worker in Switzerland who, if necessary, can find his lunch in the garden, his supper in the lake, and can earn his potato supply in the fall by helping his brother clear the land."[34]

Sixth, A Respect for Communitarian Limits. Kirk's favorite story authored by the English agrarian G. K. Chesterton was "The Yellow Bird." In it, an anarchist philosopher "liberates" a canary from its cage and a fish from its bowl. Both animals die. The lesson was that radical individualism would destroy the very limits that make life and happiness possible.[35] Kirk called for the rebuilding of real communities. Referring again to the quintessential Michigan industrial town, he wrote: "Flint will never be made a decent place to live, or a safe one, by Manchesterian [economic] doctrines, preached in all their rigidity; but Flint may be civilized by a restoration of community." In this quest for community, Kirk anticipated the "new urbanism" and urged intellectual and political leaders "to turn the amorphous modern city into a series of neighborhoods, with common interests, amenities, and economic functions." He also praised the Roman Catholic Church for having shown, uniquely among the Christian denominations, "a consistent and intelligent appreciation of the necessity for true community."[36]

Seventh, A Regard for the Attachment of Man to Soil and Property. The contemporary agrarian Berry yearns "with a kind of homesickness" for the "naturalness of a highly diversified, multi-purpose landscape, democratically divided" and "hospitable to the wild lives of plants and animals and to the wild play of human children."[37] Kirk anticipated and shared these sentiments. He agreed with Edmund Burke's depiction of Jacobinism as "the revolt of the enterprising talents of a nation against its property,"[38] with his sympathies clearly lying with property. Kirk admired the economics of the physiocrats, who combined respect for "free economic competition" and "free trade" with the agrarian view that "society's real wealth comes from the land."[39] And he urged direct action to restore vital rural life:

> The conservative will do everything in his power to prevent the further diminution of our rural population, he will recommend the decentralization of industry and the deconcentration of population, he will seek to keep as many men and women as possible to the natural and customary world in which tradition flourishes.

Kirk added:

> If we were to apply half as much energy and thought to the preservation of rural life and the old structure of community as we have to consolidation, we might be as well balanced in these relations as in Switzerland.[40]

Eighth, A Wariness Toward War. Randolph had noted that the agriculturalist bore the brunt of war and taxation.[41] In January 1941, ten months before the Japanese attack on Pearl Harbor, Davidson warned against America entering the war in Europe. Such intervention would only feed the Roosevelt administration's "highly industrialized, centralized, and socialistic order." He added: "I should have thought agrarians and decentralists would oppose our entry into the conflict when such, no matter what results might be achieved in Europe, would probably be ruinous to their hopes for a healthy reconstruction in America."[42] Kirk shared these views. He opposed American entry into the war; he believed that President Roosevelt was maneuvering the nation into the European conflict; he denounced the peacetime military draft as "slavery"; after Pearl Harbor, he was furious over the federal government's internment of Japanese Americans in concentration camps; and in 1944, he actually voted for the Socialist Party's Norman Thomas, in gratitude for his prewar, anti-imperialist speeches.[43] All the same, Kirk was not a pacifist. Drafted in 1942, he served honorably for nearly four years in the Chemical Warfare Service. He blamed the Vietnam War debacle on the Caesarism of Lyndon B. Johnson. All the same, when asked in 1968 by incoming President Richard Nixon what to do about Vietnam, Kirk urged "going to Haiphong": that is, an escalation of the war involving the mining of North Vietnam's chief harbor.[44] However, Kirk opposed the first Gulf War of 1991, largely due to the destruction of small places that it entailed. As he wrote (describing himself in the third person): ". . . Kirk would come to detest [George H. W.] Bush for his carpet-bombing of the Cradle of Civilization with its taking of a quarter of a million lives in Iraq."[45]

And ninth, A Deep Attachment to One Small Place. Writing to John C. Calhoun, Randolph had once declared that "the love of country is nothing more than the love of every man for his wife, child or friend."[46] Berry sees the social order composed, not of nations, but of "the planet's millions of human and natural neighborhoods, each on its millions of small pieces and parcels of land, each one of which is in some precious way different from all the others."[47] Kirk was a firm believer in this local patriotism. As Kirk's autobiography simply relates: "he remained rooted in Mecosta."[48] Some writers, trying to be kind, have described this village and its environs as "beautiful" or "lovely." In fact, they were neither. This was the Michigan "stump country," where great forests had been brought down to feed the lumber and furniture mills of Grand Rapids and beyond. Kirk's landscape lay stripped and bare; his village in decline; nonetheless, he loved them because this was his place, an ancestral home embracing memories and obligations. One visitor to Kirk's house at Piety Hill likened it to Rivendell, the fictional home of Elrond Halfelven in Tolkien's *Lord of the Rings.* Called "the last Homely House," Piety Hill—like Rivendell—was "a place of learning, of merriment and quiet, beside a running stream, deep in a forest-clad northern valley."[49] Father Ian Boyd ably captures the harmony that existed between Kirk's public work and his private domain in the tiny village of Mecosta:

> . . . the happy domestic life at Piety Hill was a sort of extension of his written work, a lived parable which illuminated everything he wrote

about the primacy of private life over public life, about the family as the essential human community, and about the basic loyalty to the villages, neighborhoods, and regions in which human beings were most likely to find fulfillment and a measure of happiness.[50]

Father Boyd adds that Kirk lived under a "sacramental faith," where one finds God in earthly realities. Kirk gave attention to the little things in and around Piety Hill, because he "understood the truth that ever since the Incarnation, material things are luminous and transparent rather than opaque, because it is through them that one can sometimes catch a glimpse of God."[51]

Like many others before me, I was privileged to spend some days with Kirk at Piety Hill. My eldest daughter, then ten years old, came along. It was a Rivendell experience: excellent private conversations; time to walk, read, and think alone; formal dinners with interesting guests each night; and—as my daughter will never forget—ghost stories told by Kirk before the fireplace after dinner. An openness to magic and the supernatural rooted in the stories of ancestors and grounded in a vital family home: this is the purest expression of the agrarian ideal.[52]

In these ways, Kirk was an agrarian at least as much as he was a conservative. Or perhaps one could say that Kirk's conservatism was actually agrarianism painted on a larger canvas. Avoiding the missteps of Yankee agrarians such as Bailey, Kirk was a "Northern" Agrarian only in the sense that his beloved, but *not* objectively lovely, place on earth was in the "stump country" of west-central Michigan. His rural sympathies clearly drew on the best instincts of Jefferson, Randolph, Calhoun, Weaver, Brownson, and the Twelve Southerners. It was a mindset illustrating, in Kirk's own words, "the truth that conservatism is something deeper than mere defense of shares and dividends, something nobler than mere dread of what is new."[53]

Notes

1. Russell Kirk, *The Sword of the Imagination* (Grand Rapids, MI: William B. Eerdmans, 1995), 178.
2. Jeffrey O. Nelson, "McCarthy, Eugene J. (1916–2005)," in *American Conservatism: An Encyclopedia*, ed. Bruce Frohnen, Jeremy Beer, and Jeffrey O. Nelson, (Wilmington, DE: ISI Books, 2006), 552.
3. In Annette Kirk, "Life with Russell Kirk," Russell Kirk Memorial Lecture at The Heritage Foundation, November 17, 1995; at http://users.etown.edu/m/mcdonaldw/ANNETTE.htm (1/23/2007), 4.
4. L. H. Bailey, *What is Democracy?* (Ithaca, NY: The Comstock Publishing Company, 1918), 95–96, 99.

5. Russell Kirk, "Jefferson and the Faithless," *The South Atlantic Quarterly* 40 (July 1941): 226–27.

6. Kirk, "Jefferson and the Faithless," 227.

7. Russell Kirk, "Introduction to the Transaction Edition," in *Regionalism and Nationalism in the United States: The Attack on Leviathan*, ed. Donald Davidson (New Brunswick, NJ: Transaction, 1991), viii.

8. Kirk, *The Sword of Imagination*, 176.

9. Russell Kirk, *John Randolph of Roanoke* (Indianapolis, IN: Liberty Press, 1978 [1951]), 123, 128, 131.

10. Kirk, *The Sword of Imagination*, 173.

11. Russell Kirk, *The Conservative Mind: From Burke to Eliot. Seventh Revised Edition* (Chicago and Washington, DC: Regnery Books, 1986 [1953]), 245.

12. In Clyde N. Wilson, "Russell Kirk's 'Southern Valor,'" *The Intercollegiate Review* 29 (Fall 1994), 46.

13. Kirk, "Introduction," xviii.

14. Kirk, *John Randolph of Roanoke*, 127.

15. Russell Kirk, *Economics: Work and Prosperity* (Pensacola, FL: A Beka Books, 1989), 305.

16. Quoted in: David Frum, "The Legacy of Russell Kirk," *The New Criterion* (December 13, 1994); at http://newcriterion.com/archive/13/dec94/frum.htm (1/23/2007), 3.

17. Arthur Vershiris, "Strip Malls across the Fruited Plain," *The American Conservative* (May 5, 2003); at http://www.amconmag.com/05_05_03/print/article2print.html (1/23/2007), 2.

18. John Crowe Ransom, "Reconstructed but Unregenerate," in *I'll Take My Stand: The South and the Agrarian Tradition* (Baton Rouge and London: Louisiana University Press, 1977 [1930]), 15.

19. Kirk, *John Randolph of Roanoke*, 124.

20. In: George Nash, *The Conservative Intellectual Movement in America Since 1945* (New York: Basic Books, 1976), 69.

21. Quoted in Frum, "The Legacy of Russell Kirk," 4.

22. Russell Kirk, *A Program for Conservatives* (Chicago: Regnery, 1954), 147–48.

23. Kirk, *Economics*, 305.

24. Kirk, "Introduction," ix.

25. Wendell Berry, *Remembering: A Novel* (San Francisco, CA: North Point Press, 1988), 96.

26. *I'll Take My Stand*, xxxix–xlvii.

27. Kirk, *A Program for Conservatives*, 143–47.

28. Ibid., 154–55.

29. Kirk, *The Conservative Mind*, 161.

30. See: Maclin Horton, "Prospects for Folks [A Review of Kirk's *Prospects for Conservatives*]," in *Caelum et Terra*; at http://www.caelumetterra.com/cet_backissues/article.cfm?ID=48 (1/23/2007), 3.

31. Kirk, *A Program for Conservatives*, 151, 161–62.

32. Louis Bromfield, *Pleasant Valley* (New York: Harper & Brothers, 1944), 57.

33. Bruce Frohnen, "Russell Kirk on Cultivating the Good Life," *The Intercollegiate Review* 29 (Fall 1994): 63.

34. Kirk, *A Program for Conservatives*, 162, 153.
35. Noted in Ian Boyd, "Russell Kirk: An Integrated Man," *The Intercollegiate Review* 29 (Fall 1994): 19.
36. Kirk, *A Program for Conservatives*, 156–62.
37. Wendell Berry, *A Continuous Harmony: Essays, Cultural and Agricultural* (San Diego, CA and New York: Harcourt Brace Jovanovich, 1972, 1970), 103–5.
38. Kirk, *The Program for Conservatives*, 141.
39. Kirk, *Economics*, 30.
40. Kirk, *A Program for Conservatives*, 308–9.
41. Kirk, *John Randolph of Roanoke*, 149.
42. In: "Decentralization: The Outlook for 1941. A Symposium of Opinion," *Free America* 5 (January 1941): 11–12.
43. Nash, *The Conservative Intellectual Movement in America*, 71.
44. Kirk, *The Sword of Imagination*, 300, 303, 322–23.
45. Ibid., 465.
46. Kirk, *The Conservative Mind*, 164.
47. Wendell Berry, *What Are People For?* (San Francisco: North Point Press, 1990), 200.
48. Kirk, *The Sword of Imagination*, 195.
49. Ibid., 344.
50. Boyd, "Russell Kirk: An Integrated Man," 18.
51. Ibid., 19, 22.
52. See, for example: Bromfield, *Pleasant Valley*, 60–61, 79.
53. Kirk, *The Conservative Mind*, 184.

Movements Home

8

Family-Centered
Neighborhoods

The fundamental problem facing the natural family is in fact the problem of living in cities, of housing.

Over the grand sweep of human history, in all parts of the world, the normal circumstance was that persons worked and lived in the same place. The Neolithic Revolution of a millennia ago involving the permanent settlement of land, the turn to agriculture, and the rise of towns also meant that the vast majority of people would be peasant farmers or artisans, where their places of work and their homes were one.

The family found a particularly natural home on the small farm. Meanwhile, town dwellers became artisans such as potters, blacksmiths, and wheelwrights or small-scale merchants, in both cases with shops commonly on street level and with living quarters behind or above. Men and women specialized in tasks according to their distinctive gifts. As in the country, these homes also had their kitchen gardens and chicken coops, made their own candles, crafted their own clothing. Children helped their parents in the shops and gardens and developed a life of play on the streets.

Again, with relatively few exceptions, this sort of existence was the human norm for thousands of years and hundreds of generations. We might even say that human beings were created or conditioned for this way of living.

However, the Industrial Revolution shattered it, in sweeping fashion. At its core, industrialism's upheaval exaggerated the division of labor and severed the workplace from the home. The incentives of the new industrial economy rapidly scattered family members—mothers, fathers, and children alike—into new institutions organized on industrial principles: factories; offices; schools; and reformatories. Stripped of their many former economic functions, homes became little more than shared sleeping quarters. Economic historian Karl Polanyi calls this change "The Great Transformation."[1]

Living arrangements conditioned by the union of work and home dissolved. A host of problems followed, most involving questions of family and home: Who will care for the children? What should we do with the aged? How should we treat marriage, which no longer has a firm economic base? How should we accommodate the innate differences between women and men? Why even have children, who instead of being productive helpers have now become expensive luxuries? What sort of living arrangements are best suited to urban-industrial life?

Several sets of answers have come forward over the last 150 years, answers involving five or six generations of experimentation in life under the regime of industry. I will begin by examining three of these experiments, assessing their respective theories of history and community, and pointing to their common weakness. I will also propose a fourth set of answers, which I believe shows true promise for a more family-friendly form of habitation in this new century and millennium.

The Suburban Experiment

Deep dissatisfactions over the nature of the American suburb have inspired thousands of literary denunciations. One of my favorites comes from John Keats, writing in 1960 for *The Atlantic Monthly*: "Apple Drive, like most [suburban] developments, is a jail of the soul, a wasteland of look-a-like boxes stuffed with look-alike neighbors. Here there are no facilities for human life, other than bedrooms and bathrooms. Here is a place that lacks the advantages of both city and country but retains the *dis*advantages of each. Each suburban family is somehow a broken home."[2] However, the seemingly random nature of modern suburban sprawl and the incoherence of home design commonly found there obscure the historical reality that American suburbia once actually rested on a coherent worldview. This ideology, if you will forgive that word, contained an interpretation of history with clear normative assumptions about the proper social order.

The suburban ideology grew out of the nineteenth century conflict between an agrarian, village-oriented America and the emerging urban-industrial order. Early ideologists of the American suburb included Harriet Beecher Stowe and her sister, Catharine Beecher. In their 1869 book, *The American Woman's Home*, they recognized that the ancient bond between workplace and dwelling had been shattered by industrialism. They reasoned that men were irretrievably lost to the world of commerce, individualism, and competition. It fell to women to renounce competitive ways and outside labor and to construct child-centered garden homes on the urban fringe. As wives and mothers, women must transform such homes into a combination of habitat, school, and church, where altruism and love might survive in the new age. "The family state," they concluded, "is the aptest illustration of the heavenly kingdom, and in it woman is its chief minister."[3] Their ideal suburban cottage would feature gothic windows and trim, space for family worship and the home teaching of children, a home organ for hymn sings, and samplers on the walls with favorite Bible verses.

In American Catholic homes as well, according to the popular literature of the late nineteenth century, the mother became a "home hero," a woman "cloistered in her home," a "priestess of the domestic shrine" who "cultivates religion in her family and instructs her children in its truths." Catholic home architecture of the era featured private chapels and oratories, while relatively cheap lithographs of the Sacred Heart and the Holy Family became ubiquitous.[4]

The middle decades of the twentieth century saw a theoretical secularization of this breadwinner/homemaker suburban family model, with important implications for housing design. Urban planners and architects drew on the sociology of Ernest W. Burgess and Henry J. Locke, who argued that as the American family shed its former legal and economic functions, it reorganized on the principle of companionship. While industry and government absorbed the old family tasks of home production, education, financial security, and youth training, the new "companionship [or companionate] family" would focus on "the mutual affection, the sympathetic understanding, and the comradeship of its members."[5]

According to urban planner John Dean, writing in 1951, "it [now] becomes possible . . . to maintain family interaction without recourse to the traditional housekeeping dwelling unit inherited from the family farm."[6] Architect Svend Reimer agreed, arguing that "the goal of home construction lies in the social dimension: it is a frictionless family life." This meant, he said, that formal rooms such as a parlor or single-purpose dining room should be abandoned. There was also much less need for attics, sheds, storage cellars, sewing rooms, work rooms, woodshops, pantries, large kitchens, and other relics of the productive home. Instead, the psychologically intense "companionship family" needed "flexible rooms that serve the everyday life of the family and reduce household chores to the minimum;"[7] they should feature "open plans with flexible spaces . . . for nurturing."[8]

On the one hand, the new suburbs of the 1950s did display many positive qualities. According to the urban historian Michael Johns, these suburbs "joined together the classic American forces of cultural assimilation, economic mobility, and ownership of property." While shopping centers offered only impersonal exchanges and while "suburban kids did not play with cousins down the street," parents did become "involved in their children's activities and doted on them as never before." While usually giving up regular contact with extended family, "[y]oung couples made up for those losses by focusing more intensely on the [immediate] family and by linking it to all manner of religious, charitable, political, and recreational groups." Intense forms of neighboring grew common, from the coffee klatsch of the women to the sharing of mowers and tools among the men to the "bridge clubs" found everywhere.[9]

And yet, starting sometime in the 1960s, the suburbs ceased working well as communities. Key changes involved family life. Most dramatically, marital fertility fell by 40 percent between 1960 and 1977: young children—the very purpose of suburban life—were much fewer now. The number of divorces soared. Suburban home architecture turned inward: sidewalks disappeared; garages swelled in size, soon dominating front yards; living and dining rooms shriveled still further. In another major change, suburban mothers abandoned the Beecher model of full-time motherhood, taking jobs outside the home. Where only 10 percent of suburban mothers with preschoolers worked in 1960, about 75 percent did by 1990. The suburban home had been designed around the full-time homemaker. As she disappeared, an eerie silence spread over the daylight ghost towns of late twentieth century suburbia.[10]

The Socialist Model

A second experiment in housing during the industrial age, one best labeled socialist, emerged in Sweden during the 1930s. The chief ideologist here was the social activist Alva Myrdal, joined by architect Sven Markelius. They, too, brought with them a distinctive worldview that included a clear interpretation of history and a new normative vision of the family that should drive city planning and housing design.

Who was Alva Myrdal? She may be best known today for winning the Nobel Peace Prize in 1982, awarded for her engagement on disarmament issues. However, much of her early life's work focused on matters of family and children. She was born Alva Reimer in January 1902. Her father was by profession a master carpenter. By persuasion, he was an ardent socialist, atheist, sexual radical, and feminist, views which he passed on to his daughter.

At age seventeen, she met her future husband, Gunnar Myrdal. Married in 1924, they resided in Stockholm where Gunnar worked on his doctorate in economics at The University of Stockholm. The couple cultivated a broad circle of friends, Stockholm's young intelligentsia: radicals all. And it *was* an exciting time to be on the radical democratic left. The Old Europe of the Kaisers, Tsars, Emperors, and Caliphs had been smashed by the Great War. Conservatism was everywhere discredited. Christianity was in retreat. Technology was ascendant. All things seemed possible. The Myrdals' apartment became a kind of idea salon, where young economists, historians, architects, and industrial designers met weekly to debate radical politics into the wee hours, "while consuming lots of aquavit and whiskey."[11]

The Myrdals' most productive intellectual collaboration came through their friendships with the architects, urban planners, and designers who organized the Stockholm Exposition of 1930. These men combined the architectural functionalism sweeping through Germany and France with Swedish folk design to produce the style that would later be called "Swedish modern." The architects and designers summarized their ideological purposes in the official book of the Stockholm Exposition, *Acceptera* (or in English, "Accept!").

The group saw industrialized Europe—or "A-Europe" in their terms—forming a grand circle from Stockholm to Florence and from Glasgow to Budapest. Swedish culture, art, and architecture—still mostly bound to the old rural world—faced a radical imperative to adjust to this new Europe, or become a relic. "Accept this reality," the architects declared, for "only through that do we have the chance to control events, to have the power to alter reality and shape a culture that is a flexible instrument for life."

They derided existing housing designs as uneconomical and mindlessly decorative. They insisted that art and architecture abandon the agrarian and village ideals forever, and embrace the industrialized city. The group projected "[f]ree, independent, living art work in place of sweetly pretty, gushing, valueless decoration; in place of 'elegance.'" Their aesthetic vision would combine the radical, the rational, and the hygienic and would extend beyond exterior building design to furniture, light fixtures, tableware, glassware, and even door knobs.[12]

Writing for a related volume, *Architecture and Society*, Gregor Paulsson said that it was the task of architects to engineer a "classless city" that would remove the visual and human scars of industrialization. Housing should no longer reflect class structure. Rather, architects should pursue the goal of "a total democratization of the bourgeois garden suburb."[13]

These were the themes that Alva Myrdal adapted to the design of her "Collective House" in 1932, in collaboration with Markelius. Myrdal's arguments in favor of the project rested on her view of social history. She said that the common phrase, "the family is the cell of society," incorrectly implied that the family was a stable institution. Torn away from its agrarian and artisan economic roots, she continued, the Swedish family had now ceased to be a productive household unit. Indeed, the family had evolved to a new form. Cries by reactionary politicians for a return to the traditional family and statements that "a woman's place is in the home" now rang hollow. Instead, the "traditional family" was increasingly sterile, evidenced in Sweden's plummeting birthrate and single-child homes.[14] Alva Myrdal even suggested that the "modern miniature family" spawned by industrialism had become an "abnormal" setting for children.[15]

Housing design must adjust to new social realities, she added. "[W]ork, productive work [outside the home], is now a woman's demand, and as such a social fact." Myrdal continued: "Birth control is also a social fact," which must be taken account in restructuring the home. In addition, she said that toddlers needed up to six hours a day with other children their age "so that children shall be raised to be effective members of society, not overexcited homebodies."[16]

This understanding of social history and current needs, she concluded, pointed toward construction of a Collective- or Community-House. Management of the structure would be through the semi-public Swedish cooperative, *Hyresgaesternas sparkasse- och byggnadsfoerening* (HSB). The building, with eight floors, would be placed in a park-like setting that provided ample play areas and sunshine for children. Central corridors would link family units. These units would include a closet, bathroom, "dumb waiter," cupboard space, and bedrooms for the adults and older children. There would be a central kitchen where all food would be prepared using rational restaurant procedures. It would either be delivered to the family units via "dumb waiter" or served in a community dining hall. Lounges would be constructed for discussions, meetings, and games. Community reading rooms would allow for study. There would also be collective sunrooms, gyms, storage rooms, and telephone centers.

Most important would be the community nursery. In the infants' section, children under age two could be cared for up to twenty-four hours a day by paid "competent attendants . . . in the most hygienic conditions." The toddler section would care for children ages two to six, providing day care in a well-lit playroom with "safe, pedagogically correct playthings" and "staffed with highly trained personnel." This nursery, Myrdal said, would give children needed peer-group contact, outdoor play, nutritious meals, and proper psychological attention.[17]

Markelius reasoned that this community style of living would save money, increase efficiency, promote good health, and support working mothers. Pointing to Sweden's low birthrate, he contended that this Community House would also eliminate the need for women to choose between working and bearing children. He stated that "the existence of such community houses should increase [the birth rate], especially within the professional class."[18]

Two years later, Alva Myrdal—in a book co-authored with husband Gunnar—ably summarized how this new family model resting on collectivized functions fit into the industrial world:

> In the new family . . . the wife will stand as a comrade with her husband in productive labor. . . . During working hours, . . . the family will be divided to accommodate the broader division of labor in industrialized society: working adults must be at their jobs; the children must play, eat, sleep, and go to school. Shared housing, shared free time, together with that elusive, subtle personal bond that is, we believe, a constituent element of the family will remain. However, maintaining a private household, individualistic parental authority, and the sheltered life of the housewife will not remain. They must be eliminated to allow the family's adaptation to new social developments.[19]

On a reduced scale, the Myrdal-Markelius Collective House opened in Stockholm in February 1936.

Beyond the obvious differences in physical design, the key contrast between the American suburban vision and the Myrdal "Collective House" vision was over sociology. Both were reactions to the disruption of agrarian homes by industrialization, yet each advanced a different solution. The American suburban model surrendered the father as breadwinner to the new economic order, while reorienting the home around the nurture of children. Mother would remain as a full-time "generalist" in the home, defying at least some aspects of the industrial process. In contrast, the Myrdal Collective House assumed that *both* husband and wife, *both* mother and father, would be in the full-time labor force, and that industrial techniques would spread into *all* aspects of life, including the care of infants and toddlers and meal preparation. By providing facilities for collective childcare and meal preparation, housing design itself consummated this complete victory of industrialism over the old family economy.

Rediscovering the Village

Somewhat later, a third response to industrialization also emerged: a rediscovery of the village. In her famed 1961 book, *The Death and Life of Great American Cities*, Jane Jacobs combined profound insights with common sense to skewer the urban planners and redevelopers of her day. These experts, using theories not far removed from the Myrdal-Markelius collectivist model, were tearing down old neighborhoods in New York, Chicago, and Boston, and building in their place huge public housing complexes. The latter commonly combined modernist high-rise apartments with parks and green space where the children would supposedly play.

In practice, though, these playgrounds became centers of gang violence and other forms of anti-social behavior, posing special threats to the young. Real children avoided them. Jacobs showed that even the supposed child-friendly "courtyards" in the projects failed: as she explained, "no child of enterprise or spirit will willingly stay in such a boring place after he reaches the age of six."[20]

Noting that most of the urban planners of her day were men, Jacobs pointed to another oddity: "They [actually] design and plan to *ex*clude men as part of normal, daytime family wherever people live. In planning residential life, they aim at filling the presumed daily needs of impossibly vacuous housewives and preschool tots." In short, their design principles would inevitably produce "matriarchal societies," where responsible men would be largely absent.[21] Indeed, life in the urban projects *was* rapidly devolving into the domain of the unmarried mother and effectively fatherless children.

Jacobs' response was to recover the urban village. In a sense, she held that properly planned cities were not hostile to family life. Many of the old neighborhoods, she argued, had been decent and happy places which effectively sheltered families and protected children through a vital street life.

Fittingly, her model was Greenwich *Village*, a section of Manhattan that had retained a pleasing form of mixed use: low-rise residences side-by-side with shops, cafes, and professional offices. Most important, though, were the sidewalks. She called them "uniquely vital and irreplaceable organs of city safety, public life, and child-rearing." The ideal sidewalk would be thirty to thirty-five feet wide, a space that could accommodate shade trees, pedestrians, adult street life, old-fashioned loitering (which she praised), and the play of children. Regarding the latter, she noted:

> They slop in puddles, write with chalk, jump rope, roller skate, shoot marbles, trot out their possessions, converse, trade cards, play stoopball, walk stilts, decorate soap-box scooters, dismember old baby carriages, climb on railings.

All this occurred under the watchful eyes of dozens of adults: neighbors and shopkeepers as well as parents. Part of the charm for children, Jacobs added, was "the accompanying sense of freedom to roam up and down the sidewalks," learning self-reliance under the watchful eye of an urban village.[22]

The so-called New Urbanism derives from Jacobs' work to a considerable degree. The New Urbanists are architects and urban planners who see themselves as renewing the "traditions of human settlement that emerged over the millennia." They explain "that human settlements have traditionally been oriented toward the pedestrian and . . . that the neighborhood is the fundamental unit of human settlement." They define a true neighborhood in terms of time: a walk from the center of a neighborhood to its edge should take only five minutes. Even a rural village, they say, should be understood as "essentially a single, free standing neighborhood in the country."

A good New Urbanist neighborhood features: a discernable center and clear edges; shops and offices within walking distance which meet most of the residents' basic needs; places that "symbolize community identity" such as school, civic buildings, and park; large sidewalks with shade trees; and residences that face the street, have a discernable entrance, and a functional front porch.[23]

Over the last two decades, hundreds of New Urbanist developments have mushroomed in the United States. With names like Mashpee

Commons, Santana Row, and Blue Back Square, these projects offer families opportunities to reclaim at least some aspects of village life, within an urban setting.

However, relative to families, a disturbing note has also been sounded in recent years. A number of New Urbanist projects have sought to restrict, or prohibit, the presence of children. Sometimes, it is the developers' wish for adult-only or retirement housing; other times, it is public officials seeking to avoid the financial burden of educating more children. As New Urbanist writer Philip Langdon notes in his essay, "Don't Want No Short People": "Mixed-use, pedestrian-oriented [retail] centers have been a logical response . . . to the dullness and obsolescence of the uninspired conventional [shopping] centers." Yet, "[w]hat good is a town center if it excludes its freshest, least jaded inhabitants," the children?[24]

Also relative to families and children, an interesting variation of the New Urbanism is called cohousing. The idea of building community through cohousing emerged in Denmark during the 1970s, and came to America through the advocacy of Kathryn McCamant and Charles Durrett. As to location, cohousing projects are quite adaptable: from abandoned factory, or "brownfield," sites in central cities to exurban locales in the countryside. They usually involve twenty to forty residence units around shared open space with a prominent common house. While quite open to children, cohousing advocates insist that they "espouse no ideology," nor target any particular family type.[25] And, broadly speaking, this seems to be true. According to news reports, for example, cohousing enthusiasts include both stay-at-home wives and mothers[26] and aging gay women.[27] Cohousing so distinguishes itself from "intentional communities" that build on a common political ideology, social vision, or shared religion.

All the same, the cohousing movement might be seen as a *compromise* between the "suburban" and "collective" models that I described earlier. Where the contemporary suburban home is strenuously "private" and the Myrdal house largely collectivized, the prominent common building found in a cohousing neighborhood provides opportunities for group interaction and shared tasks on a flexible basis. Where the Myrdal house was organized as a cooperative without true ownership, cohousing residents commonly own their homes, as found in the suburbs. Where the collective kitchen and nursery of the Myrdal house used paid specialists to provide community food and child care, a cohousing neighborhood normally relies on volunteer or exchange labor to prepare group dinners and to care for the toddlers, creating a different dynamic.

Where the suburban home was built around the fulltime homemaker and the Collective House around universal adult employment, the cohousing neighborhood aspires to satisfy and support both the parent-at-home and the working mother. As one of the former reports: "Stay-at-home moms often feel isolated and overwhelmed when their children are little. In a cohousing project like ours, there are always people around to offer help and provide female company."[28] And a cohousing profile of "Anne," a working mother, explains: "Instead of frantically trying to put together a nutritious dinner, Anne can relax now, spend some time with her children, and then eat with her family in the common house."[29] Assuming such reports are representative, these are encouraging results.

The key to cohousing success seems to lie in the rigorous planning and design process and in ongoing community governance, where numerous meetings, long discussions, and decisions by consensus drive out the uncommitted and the troublemakers and also create levels of openness, mutual awareness, and trust that make community living possible. Not the typical American suburban environment, or the Myrdal Collective House model, or a conventional New Urbanist development have had mechanisms in place to construct this new sort of "village mentality."

The Function-Rich Home

And yet, I would argue that there exists a common weakness and lost opportunity in all these models. Suburban America, the Myrdal Collective House, the New Urbanism, and even cohousing communities all accept as a given the radical separation of work and home introduced by industrialization. Each approach looks for ways to reassemble family homes shorn of productive functions. All accept and accommodate industrialism, rather than challenge it; all accept the weakened, nonproductive family as a given.

The truly exciting prospect for the twenty-first century actually lies in the opportunity to undo the industrial revolution at least in certain ways, and to the benefit of the natural family. Even cohousing advocates seem to forget that the *true* pre-industrial village was more than a place to eat, sleep, and recreate. As noted at the outset, the authentic village was also a place to work, to make things, and to provide services.

Jane Jacobs had a sense of this. In pointing to the matriarchies emerging in the urban housing projects of her time, she commented:

115

"*Working places* . . . must be mingled right in with residences if men . . . are to be around city children in daily life." Today, she would add "women" as well. Jacobs also blasted planning and zoning that insisted on "segregating dwellings from work," calling instead for "conditions that stimulate minglings"[30] of places of employment next to homes. In my view, she simply did not take the last step: moving employment back *into* the home.

Such a counter-revolution is already well-advanced in America. It can be seen in:

- *home schools*, where the educational function—after 150 years of operating on an industrial model—has returned to the hearth for well over two million American children.
- *home businesses*, most of them encouraged and sustained by the great new commercial democracy of the Internet, which are becoming the digital equivalent of the old artisan's shop; by one count, over thirty million home businesses may now exist in America, the majority run by women.
- *telecommuting*, which means that even large commercial enterprises of a certain sort can go "virtual," ranging from magazine publishing to brokerages to medical record-keeping to product design to higher education.

Similar technological gifts of the digital age open prospects for the return of professional offices to homes; among dentists, family doctors, lawyers, and the like. The external barriers to this today are artificial: stifling professional rules; zoning laws; and restrictive housing covenants. These can all be changed, most easily for new developments.

In short, current urban planners and architects have an unprecedented opportunity to create an integrated form of living that would substantially heal the great breach between work and home, so restoring human beings to their natural habitat. To architects and urban planners, I simply urge: Design homes in neighborhoods that are also schools and places of enterprise; with schoolrooms, workrooms, home offices, and small shops, along with the garden. Such an achievement would help end the gender wars of our age, greatly improve the lives of children, strengthen marriages, energize neighborhoods, and even lighten the carbon footprints of everyone involved. For families, it would mark a true homecoming.

We can actually imagine the lonely contemporary American suburbs reborn, with small shops where ghostly living rooms once stood;

with lawyers, doctors, and dentists again working out of home offices, assisted by able young apprentices; with productive gardens and modest animal life; and with the midday laughter of home-schooled children where silence had recently prevailed.

And in the cities, we can also imagine vital neighborhoods once again alive with the chatter and noise of the young, reintegrating commerce and other necessary work with the daily lives of families: mothers and fathers, boys and girls: the authentic village, reborn.

Notes

1. Karl Polanyi, *The Great Transformation* (New York: Farrar & Rinehart, 1944), 1–2.
2. John Keats, "Compulsive Suburbia," *The Atlantic Monthly* 205 (April 1960): 47–50.
3. Catharine Beecher and Harriet Beecher Stowe, *The American Woman's Home, or Principles of Domestic Science* (New York: J. B. Ford, 1869), Chapter 1.
4. Colleen McDannell, *The Christian Home in Victorian America, 1840–1900* (Bloomington: Indiana University Press, 1986), 56–58, 66, 75, 137–40.
5. E. W. Burgess and H. J. Locke, *The Family* (New York: American Book Company, 1945), 651–72.
6. John P. Dean, "Housing Design and Family Values," *Land Economics* 29 (May 1953): 128–41.
7. Svend Reimer, "Architecture for Family Living," *Journal of Social Issues* 7 (1951): 140–51.
8. Gertrude Sipperly Fish, ed., *The Story of Housing* (New York: Macmillan, 1979), 476–78.
9. Michael Johns, *Moment of Grace: The American City in the 1950's* (Berkely: University of California Press, 2003), 94–98.
10. See: Nicholas Lemann, "Stressed Out in Suburbia," *The Atlantic* 264 (November 1989), 40–43.
11. See: Yvonne Hirdman, "Utopia in the Home," *International Journal of Political Economy* 22 (1992): 30.
12. Gunnar Asplund et al, *Acceptera* (Stockholm: Tidens förlag, 1931), 16–25, 119, 171, 186–88, 198.
13. Gregor Paulsson, "Arkitektur och politik," in *Arkitektur och samhälle*, ed. Gregor Paulsson et al, (Stockholm: Broderna Lagerström, 1932), 15.
14. Alva Myrdal, "Kollektiv bostadsform," *Tiden* 24 (December 1932): 602.
15. Alva Myrdal, "Kollektivhuset," *Hertha* (January 1933): 126.
16. Alva Myrdal, "Kollektiv bostadsform," 602; and Alva Myrdal, "Yrkeskvinnans barn," *Yrkes—Kvinnor Klubbnytt* (February 1933): 63.
17. Sven Markelius, "Kollektivhuset," in *Arkitektur och sämhalle*, ed. Gregor Paulsson.
18. From a lecture by Markelius before the Working Women's Club of Stockholm; reported in *Svenska Dagbladet*, December 9, 1932.
19. Alva and Gunnar Myrdal, *Kris i befolkiningsfrågan* (Stockholm: Bonniers, 1934), 319.

20. Jane Jacobs, *The Death and Life of Great American Cities* (New York: Random House, 1961), 75–80.

21. Jacobs, *The Death and Life of Great American Cities*, 83–84.

22. Ibid., 86–87.

23. Benjamin E. Northrup and Benjamin J. Bruxvoort Lipscomb, "Country and City: The Common Vision of Agrarians and New Urbanists," in *The Essential Agrarian Reader*, ed. Norman Wirzba (Lexington: The University of Kentucky Press, 2003), 191–211.

24. Philip Langdon, "Don't Want No Short People," *New Urban News* 13 (March 2008): 2.

25. Kathryn McCamant and Charles Durrett, "Building a CoHousing Community [1989];" at http://www.context.org/ICLIB/IC21/McCamant.htm, 2–3.

26. Danielle Crawford Skov, "The New Neighborhood: CoHousing and Families," *Mothering: Natural Family Living* 111 (March/April 2002).

27. Marsha King, "Elder Co-Housing Project is Aimed at Gay Women," *The Seattle Times* (June 17, 2007).

28. Skov, "The New Neighborhood;" and Aminatta Forna, "CoHo: The Ultimate Nineties Lifestyle," *The (London) Independent* (September 7, 1997).

29. McCamant and Durrett, "Building a CoHousing Community," 3.

30. Jacobs, *The Death and Life of Great American Cities*, 84, 175.

9

Patriarchs Triumphant?

Aspiring patriarchs would seem to have little to cheer about in recent decades. Equal pay statutes have destroyed the "family wage" regime that once rewarded the breadwinning father as "head of household." The real hourly wages of blue collar men are lower today than they were forty years ago. Title IX rules have forcibly turned much of the once male-dominated athletic world over to the women. Aggressive little boys are tamed by Ritalin. School textbooks fervently promote the feminist worldview, celebrating female steelworkers and male care-givers. The same ideology dominates the vast majority of American colleges and universities; women's studies programs are ubiquitous. The military places the quest for androgyny above the goal of victory. Prestige professions such as medical doctor and lawyer are rapidly being feminized. Marriage rates and marital birthrates are low. Child support orders turn many remaining fathers into the indentured servants of their ex-wives. Church liturgies sound like old *Ms.* magazine articles. Language police crush the generic "he."

Like all other interest groups or hobbyists in America, patriarchs did have their own journal. Issuing from tiny Willis, Virginia, *Patriarch* magazine sought "nothing less than a return to patriarchy, a society led by strong, godly men. . . . Each man should aim to be the founder of a dynasty for God."[1] However, its editor suspended publication in 2004; circulation was probably never more than a few thousand; and in terms of graphics, it was clearly the product of a simple home business. Today's would-be patriarch now has nowhere to turn for advice and inspiration.

And yet, to hear the feminists tell it, patriarchs remain wily and clever foes; their power undiminished. Feminist historian Judith Bennett marvels at patriarchy "in all its immense variety."[2] The Marxist Heidi Hartmann finds patriarchy to be "a strikingly resilient form of social organization."[3] Philosopher Gerda Lerner sees patriarchy as "remarkably adaptive and resilient."[4]

When one strategy for the suppression of women fails, it seems, the patriarchs simply craft another. For example, after women won the vote and equal property rights in the early twentieth century, the patriarchs invented Freudianism which marked those women as "neurotic" and "perverted" who were not heterosexually active. As feminist theorist Sylvia Walby concludes: "for every victory won by women there has been a patriarchal blacklash in another area. Patriarchy is a dynamic system. . . . If women do win . . . then patriarchal forces will regroup and regain control over them in other ways."[5] Might this be true?

Patriarchs and Evolution

Feminists have long obsessed over the origin of patriarchy and its key institution, the family. Early on, they found little in the then understood human record that was encouraging. During the late nineteenth century, most anthropologists saw the patriarchal family as the pinnacle of human civilization. In *Ancient Law* (1861), Sir Henry Maine said that societies with women in power were low on the evolutionary scale, a situation suited only for savages. In contrast, patriarchal rule in families and states was the culmination of human progress. John Lubbock, in *The Origin of Civilization and the Primitive Condition of Man* (1870), also celebrated male rule as the foundation of civilized living. Lewis Henry Morgan's *Ancient Society* (1877) devised an evolutionary sequence from a savage state dominated by women, through a barbaric phase with some matrilineal qualities, to civilization resting on patriarchal monogamy.

Rescuing a feminist worldview were Karl Marx and Friedrich Engels. According to the latter, Marx was planning to write a book on the family but died before starting the work. Engels took on the task, producing *The Origin of the Family, Private Property, and the State* in 1884. Drawing heavily on Morgan's *Ancient Society*, the book adopted the same evolutionary scheme, yet turned the argument on its head. Where Morgan saw patriarchy as the summit of social evolution, Engels saw only oppression:

> The overthrow of the mother right [found in savage society] was the *world historical defeat of the female sex.* The man took command in the home also; the woman was degraded and reduced to servitude; she became the slave of his lust and a mere instrument for the production of children.

Engels cast monogamous marriage as "the first class oppression." He urged a return to the social order last seen among Morgan's savages, to be achieved by easy divorce, free love, the socialized care and rearing of children, and "the reintroduction of the whole female sex into the public industries."[6]

Here was an account of history into which feminists could sink their teeth, continuing to inspire their cause to this day.[7] Later interpreters would expand the narrative. Andrea Dworkin identified two historical forms of patriarchy: "the farming mode," where a woman would be kept and exploited by one man for life; and "the brothel mode," where women obstensibly enjoyed more freedom, but lost the support of men once their sexual and reproductive periods were over.[8] Eli Zaretsky argued that while men were oppressed under capitalism by having to do wage work, women were oppressed by *not* being allowed to do wage work.[9]

Hartmann saw an even more devious patriarchy cutting a dirty deal with capitalism. Employers discovered that paying a little extra to laboring men allowed the latter to suppress their own womenfolk by keeping them at home, while the capitalists gained healthier babies who would grow into more obedient workers. In this way, "the family wage cemented the partnership between patriarchy and capital."[10] After profusely praising Engels, Lerner traced the suppression of women to the dawn of the Neolithic age, when they were "commodified": "Women themselves became a resource, acquired by men much as the land was acquired by men. Women were exchanged or bought in marriages for the benefit of their families; later, they were conquered and bought in slavery." This meant that "the enslavement of women" by protopatriarchs "preceded the formation of classes and class oppression."[11]

Other recent scholars have painted a happier face on Neolithic farming cultures, but agree that the arrival of patriarchy brought misery to women. Harvard anthropologist Marija Gimbutas claimed to find this better world on the Steppes of "Old Europe" (pre-3000 BC). Author of *The Goddessess and Gods of Old Europe*, she sees in the archeological record a "matristic" society of farmers combining matrilineal, matrifocal, matricentric, and egalitarian qualities, where the sexes were balanced and complementary; where there were no hierarchies. These communities prized figurines featuring pregnant women, which the Harvard don sees as representing a sacred cosmology within a mother-kinship social structure.

Alas, according to Gimbutas, this nearly Edenic existence was undone by the Kurgans. Over 2,500 years, three waves of these strange invaders violently introduced a new value system. Their patriarchal, hierarchal social structure featured bronze metallurgy, weapons, warfare, horse riding, and elite burials often involving human and animal sacrifices. The Kurgans also celebrated bride stealing, cattle rustling, and heroism in combat and they worshipped sky gods and male warrior gods. These patriarchal peoples were organized for "predatory expansion,"[12] which they proceeded to do, accidentally creating western civilization in the process. As with Engels, though, the presumed existence of a nonpatriarchal "golden age" in the pre-Kurgan era suggested that some form of matriarchy might be possible in the future.

"Public" Patriarchy

And yet, another batch of feminist scholars is reluctantly concluding that there will be no shining future free of the patriarchs. Rather, this wily and clever foe has taken on still another form, intent on continuing the suppression of women. They call the new strategy "public patriarchy."

Walby lays out the way in which "progressive reforms have been met with patriarchal counterattack." Specifically, feminist-inspired laws opening educational opportunities and professions to women combined with welfare benefits such as public daycare to produce a curious result:

> While [women] lose their own individual patriarch, they do not lose their subordination to other patriarchal structures and practices. Indeed, they become ever more exposed to certain of the more diffused sets of patriarchal practices.

Once dependent on a "family wage" earning husband, the woman now sees her standard of living fixed by "the patriarchal state" through welfare benefits and by "the patriarchally structured labor market." Although all major feminist goals had been achieved, "patriarchy changed in form, incorporating some of the hard won changes into new traps for women."[13]

Frances Fox Piven describes the new reality. Ever fewer women are in traditional families. For their part, men "are increasingly 'liberated' from their obligations under the moral economy of domesticity." A few working women reach top positions as doctors, lawyers, and corporate executives, but most wind up in the low-pay service sector.

More promisingly, "[w]omen have . . . developed a large and important relationship to the welfare state as the employees of [its] programs." As early as 1980, American women held 70 percent of the jobs at all levels of government concerned with social service. This represented about half of all professional jobs claimed by women. Piven accepts this public patriarchy—where women do exercise some power through "their 'dependent' relationship with the state"—as the best option available.[14]

Carole Pateman, however, retorts that Piven has simply fallen into the new trap identified by Walby. As Pateman writes: "The power and capriciousness of husbands [are] being replaced by the arbitrariness, bureaucracy, and power of the state, the very state that has upheld patriarchal power."[15]

Evidence backing Walby and Pateman's pessimistic view comes from Scandinavia, where the feminist ideology has been the most aggressively pursued. Observers have noted that in Norway, female members of parliament usually serve on the committees dealing with family, education, and social welfare; the men, meanwhile, serve on the high-prestige committees dealing with commerce, industry, and oil. In Sweden, men still overwhelmingly dominate private business; whereas female chief executive officers are almost unknown.[16]

A 2006 study of "public patriarchy" by two Israeli sociologists produced astonishing results. Using a "Welfare State Intervention Index," they examined the status of women in twenty-one developed western nations, including the Scandinavian lands, the nations of central and western Europe, Canada, the United States, and Australia. The researchers found that after four decades of intense feminist activism, men still controlled virtually all positions of prestige and power in the advanced Scandinavian welfare states, while women were still doing "women's work." As they explain:

> . . . state activities, while facilitating womens' entrance into the labor market, do not facilitate their entry into high-authority and elite positions. Rather, the very same characteristics—generous family policies and a large public service sector—seem to reproduce the gendered division of labor and, in effect, *decrease* women's chances of joining desirable positions.

Indeed, welfare states "channel women in disproportionate numbers into feminine occupational niches" such as child care, elder care, nursing, and elementary education. The odds of a woman being employed in classically "female" occupations are actually highest in Denmark, Finland, and Sweden![17] And so, just as predicted by the pessimists, the patriarchs win again: men still rule and women are, as before, still doing traditional "women's work."

On Manliness

Perhaps it would be wise to move beyond feminist constructs to explain this result. In his controversial book, *Manliness*, Harvard political philosopher Harvey Mansfield agrees with the grumbling and subdued feminists that "every previous society, including our democracy up to now, *has* been some kind of patriarchy, permeated by stubborn, self-insistent manliness." Mansfield explains the rule of men by their greater levels of aggression and assertiveness. All the same, true manliness is constructive and progressive:

> Manliness brings change or restores order at moments when routine is not enough, when the plan fails, when the whole idea of rational control by modern science develops leaks. Manliness is the next-to-last resort, before resignation and prayer.[18]

In his book *Why Men Rule* (originally titled *The Inevitability of Patriarchy*), anthropologist Steven Goldberg also underscores what honest feminist historians reluctantly admit: there never has been a matriarchy where women ruled over men; the "Amazons never existed"; and despite the occasional female leader, "suprafamilial authority is *always* overwhelmingly male." He traces these realities to the "neuro-endocrinological differences between men and women." Because of their brain structure and abundance of testosterone, men are more inclined to competitiveness and the quest for dominance: "whatever variable one chooses, authority, status, and dominance within each [social] stratum rest with the male in contact with equivalent females." Meanwhile, the neurons and hormones of women condition them for the care and rearing of the young (which he does call "the single most important function served in any society or in nature itself").[19]

In an unexpected 2006 article for the journal *Foreign Policy*, Phillip Longman of the progressive New America Foundation describes "The Return of Patriarchy." He defines this system as "a cultural regime that serves to keep birth rates high among the affluent, while also maximizing parents' investments in their children," and adds: "No advanced civilization has yet learned how to endure without it." Essential pillars of patriarchy, he says, include the stigmatization of illegitimate children and single mothers. The system also emotionally penalizes women who do not marry and have children. Moreover, since both men and women can grow weary of the burdens of patriarchy, family affirming religious faith is essential to long-term success. Considering the early twenty-first century, Longman concludes that the "great difference in fertility rates between secular individualists and religious and cultural conservatives augurs a vast, demographically driven change in modern societies." The future will belong to those who "suppress their individualism and submit to father."[20]

A Vision

Even these portraits of the inevitable patriarchal future, though, lack poetry. Both demoralized feminists and sober male analysts continue to see the family as through a glass darkly: as an arena defined by power, assertiveness, and submission. Is this the real message taught by history?

Some of the earliest histories of the social condition of women remain among the best: Dr. Eileen Powers' book on *Medieval English Nunneries* (1922) and her long essays on "The Menegier's Wife" and "The Position of Women [In the Middle Ages]"; Alice Clark's *The Working Life of Women* (1920); Ivy Pinchbeck's *Women Workers in the Industrial Revolution, 1750–1850* (1930); and Mary Beard's *Women as Force in History* (1946). They rely on solid historical procedures, including the use of account books, household diaries, letters, memoirs, court reports, church documents, and corporation and guild records. Their common tale explodes the myth that the history of women is one long saga of subjugation. Rather, as Ferdinand Lundberg and Marynia F. Farnham summarize in their now neglected 1948 classic, *Modern Woman: The Lost Sex*:

> [T]he hard fact is that women, prior to the vast industrial and economic changes of the eighteenth century usually described as the Industrial Revolution, had large and relatively satisfactory scope for their unquestionable energies and talents . . . [T]he all too familiar view of women suddenly emerging in the nineteenth century from a long historical night onto a sunlit [feminist] plain is completely wrong.[21]

This is to say that in addition to doing their vital and irreplaceable work of bearing and rearing the young, the women of ancient Egypt, Babylon, Greece and Rome, of the medieval era, and of Early Modern

Europe enjoyed scope for their specific talents, exercised real power, and knew high esteem.

It may clarify matters at this point to offer up the enduring natural family as an ideal. Or better still, we might turn to it as a vision, albeit one readily attainable.

This course elevates a culture that understands the marriage of a woman to a man to be the central aspiration of the young. This culture affirms marriage as the best path to health, security, and fulfillment. It affirms the home built on marriage to be the source of true political sovereignty. It also holds the household framed by marriage to be the first economic unit, a place rich in activity. This culture treasures family held private property in home and in land as the foundation of independence and liberty. It encourages young women to grow into wives, homemakers, and mothers. It encourages young men to grow into husbands, homebuilders, and fathers. This culture celebrates the marital sexual union as the unique source of human life. These homes are open to full quivers of children, the means of generational continuity, and community renewal.[22]

Call it the consequence of a patriarchal order, or call it the natural family: this model for living is attuned to human nature, and it is the arbiter of human destiny. Where the feminist sees just another trap and the scientist sees the effects of differentiated neurons and hormones, the conservative sees a rightly ordered world, where the natural complementarity of man and woman finds fulfillment; and where women are most likely to find health, wealth, happiness, and fulfillment.

The Fruits of Private Patriarchy

This latter truth is affirmed by the natural and social sciences. For example, researchers at Princeton University have found that married women in industrialized nations live longer than their unmarried peers, with the gap actually growing in recent decades.[23] Epidemiologists studying 7,500 white women aged sixty-five or older have also uncovered strong evidence that marriage lengthens women's lives; indeed, it is "the most consistent predictor" of differential mortality.[24] An article in *Social Biology* dealing with women is bluntly titled, "Perils of Single Life and Benefits of Marriage."[25]

Marriages to private or sole patriarchs also make women wealthier. Researchers at Cornell and the University of Washington have shown that "the power of marriage to deliver affluence for women is extremely strong." Marriage works this way by eliminating many of the extra household expenses that two single persons would otherwise have and by enabling "a division of labor that maximizes family income."[26] Investigators at Purdue have reported that "being married has a large effect on household wealth," with unmarried women enjoying a 63 percent reduction in total wealth over their lifetimes, when compared to their married peers. This occurs because marriage "provides institutionalized protection, which generates economies of scale, task specialization, and access to work-related fringe benefits, that lead [in turn] to rewards like broader social networks and higher savings rates."[27]

Marriages to sole patriarchs make women happier, as well. An American researcher has found that married people say they are "more satisfied in life" than unmarried people are, "regardless of gender." Feminists usually retort that wedlock benefits men more than women. However, this study showed that married women actually score higher than married men on "perception of well-being."[28] Surveying seventeen developed nations, including the United States, sociologist Steven Stack has reported "perhaps the strongest evidence to date in support of the relationship between marital status and happiness." He adds that "marriage protects females just as much from unhappiness as it protects males." Moreover, while men and women engaging in unmarried cohabitation were happier than singletons, their happiness quotient was less than one quarter of that of married persons.[29]

Finally, women are best protected from harm when sheltered by private patriarchs. Contrary to feminist theory, domestic abuse of all sorts—physical, verbal, and psychological—occurs much more often among lesbian couples than among male–female pairs. Almost half of lesbians surveyed in one study report "being or having been the victim of relationship violence." The research team even admits that "the academic community . . . shares some of the blame for ignoring same-sex domestic violence" due to "a reluctance to challenge feminist frameworks."[30] Cohabitation with a man is also much more dangerous than life with a husband. Investigators have found that cohabiting males express a more "tolerant view of rape," probably because they are "more accepting of violence and control" than married men. After factoring in household income, education, age, and occupation, another research team found cohabiting women to be nearly *five times* more likely to experience "severe violence" than their married peers.[31]

New research affirming similar points continues to pour out of the academy. University of Virginia sociologists, examining the National Survey of Families and Homes, report in a 2006 article for *Social*

Forces that women are happiest when they cleave to hearth and home and when their husbands earn at least two-thirds of family income. These women also report higher levels of quality time and emotional engagement with their husbands, when compared to women in more egalitarian marriages.[32] Australian research reported the same year in the *Journal of Sociology* shows that for mothers with children under the age of eighteen, working full-time outside the home raises the odds of being in poor health. In contrast, staying at home or only working part-time lowers their risk of sickness.[33] A 2005 study of women's mental and physical health, appearing in the *Journal of Research in Crime and Delinquency*, finds that "[m]arried women and those with more children are less likely to be very concerned about personal safety"—that is, they feel safer—when compared to single and divorced women and those having fewer children.[34] Even easy divorce, touted by feminists as a vehicle of liberation, hurts women more than men. A 2005 study appearing in *Race, Gender & Class* reports that "women are more psychologically vulnerable to marital dissolution than men, regardless of race."[35]

These affirmations of the natural family grounded in marriage involve effects among women. Another vast body of research shows similar positive consequences for men. A still larger mound of research underscores the powerful positive effects of the natural family model on children, both girls and boys. The message from the biological, medical, and social sciences is clear: children do best when they are born into and raised by their two biological parents who are married. Under any variation—be it communal, cohabiting, same sex, step parent, or sole parent households—children will predictably face more problems. They will be more likely to do poorly in school, be incarcerated, abuse alcohol and drugs, have serious health problems, and attempt suicide. They will be less likely to become happy and productive citizens.

The Choice

Patriarchy *is* inevitable, as the more gloomy of the feminist theorists have admitted. Walby summarizes: "Women are no longer restricted to the domestic hearth, but have the whole society in which to roam and be exploited."[36] She errs only in failing to recognize the real source of patriarchy and to appreciate her real choice.

As noted early in this volume, paleoanthropologists now know that even before the first hominids on the African savanna had gone bipedal, these creatures were conjugal; that is, they were pairing off in long-term bonds, where the females traded sexual exclusivity for the provisioning and protection provided by individual males. These social inventions of marriage and fatherhood—not expansion of the brain case—were the decisive steps in human evolution, and they occurred well over three million years ago.[37]

Nothing important has changed since. Women cannot successfully raise children on their own. When they try to do so in large numbers, the results are poverty, violence, and misery (for proof, simply visit the average American urban ghetto). Women need some entity that will help them secure property, gain food and clothing, and control the boys. There are only two practical options: either the private patriarch (who is, in the end, simply a contemporary form of *the husbandman* found in the agrarian past), a figure who is adept at breadwinning and taming the lads; or the public patriarch (i.e., the welfare state), which provides food stamps, public housing, and day-care subsidies and eventually jails a large share of the lads. The first choice is compatible with health, happiness, wealth creation, and political liberty. The second choice is a sure path to the servile state.

Women of the world, there is no third way here: which patriarchy do you choose?

Notes

1. Phillip H. Lancaster, "Why 'Patriarch'?" *Patriarch*, no. 36 (February 2001): 41.
2. Judith M. Bennett, *History Matters: Patriarchy and the Challenge of Feminism* (Philadelphia: University of Pennsylvania Press, 2006), 54.
3. Heidi Hartmann, "The Unhappy Marriage of Marxism and Feminism: Towards a More Progressive Union," *Capital and Class* 8 (Summer 1979): 10.
4. Gerda Lerner, *The Creation of Patriarchy* (New York: Oxford University Press, 1986), 216.
5. Sylvia Walby, *Theorizing Patriarchy* (Oxford: Basil Blackwell, 1990), 173.
6. Friedrich Engels, *The Origin of the Family, Private Property and the State*, trans. Ernest Untermann (Chicago, IL: Charles H. Kerr, 1902), 24–27, 80–82, 90–92, 99 (emphasis added).
7. See Richard Weikart, "Marx, Engels, and the Abolition of the Family," *History of European Ideas* 18, no. 5, (1994): 657.
8. Andrea Dworkin, *Right-Wing Women* (New York: Perigee, 1983).
9. Eli Zaretsky, "Capitalism, the Family, and Personal Life," *Socialist Revolution* 13–14 (January–April 1973): 114.
10. Hartmann, "The Unhappy Marriage of Marxism and Feminism," 18.
11. Lerner, *The Creation of Patriarchy*, 212–13.
12. Joan Marler, "The Beginnings of Patriarchy in Europe: Reflections on the Kurgan Theory of Marija Gimbutas," in *The Rule of Mars: Readings on the*

Origins, History and Impact of Patriarchy, ed. Cristina Biaggi (Winchester, CT: KIT, 2005), 53–61.

13. Walby, *Theorizing Patriarchy*, 174, 197, 200–201.
14. Frances Fox Piven, "Ideology and the State: Women, Power, and the Welfare State," in *Women, the State, and Welfare*, ed. Linda Gordon (Madison: The University of Wisconsin Press, 1990): 251–55.
15. Carole Pateman, "The Patriarchal Welfare State," in *Democracy and the Welfare State*, ed. Amy Gutmann (Princeton, NJ: Princeton University Press, 1988): 234.
16. Noted in Steven Goldberg, *Why Men Rule: A Theory of Male Dominance* (Chicago and LaSalle, IL: Open Court Press, 1993), 24–25.
17. Hadas Mandel and Moshe Semgonov, "A Welfare State Paradox: State Interventions and Women's Employment Opportunities in 22 Countries," *American Journal of Sociology* 111 (May 2006): 1913, 1916, 1933.
18. Harvey C. Mansfield, *Manliness* (New Haven and London: Yale University Press, 2006), ix, 58, 64.
19. Goldberg, *Why Men Rule*, 14–38, 64–66.
20. Phillip Longman, "The Return of Patriarchy," *Foreign Policy* (March/April 2006): 56–65.
21. Ferdinand Lundberg and Marynia F. Farnham, *Modern Woman: The Lost Sex* (New York and London: Harper and Brothers, 1947), 420–21.
22. These paragraphs are adapted from "A Vision," found in: Allan C. Carlson and Paul T. Mero, *The Natural Family: A Manifesto* (Dallas: Spence Publishing Company, 2007), 12–13.
23. Yuaureng Hu and Noreen Goldman, "Mortality Differentials by Marital Status: An International Comparison," *Demography* 27 (1990): 233–50.
24. Thomas Rutledge, et al., "Social Networks and Marital Status Predict Mortality in Older Women: Prospective Evidence from the Study of Osteoporotic Fractures," *Psychosomatic Medicine* 65 (2003): 688–94.
25. Ellen Eliason Kisker and Noreen Goldman, "Perils of Single Life and Benefits of Marriage," *Social Biology* 34 (1987): 135–51.
26. Thomas A. Hirschl, Joyce Altobelli, and Mark R. Rank, "Does Marriage Increase the Odds of Affluence? Exploring the Life Course Probabilities," *Journal of Marriage and Family* 65 (2003): 927–38.
27. Janet Wilmoth and Gregor Koso, "Does Marital History Matter? Marital Status and Wealth Outcomes among Preretirement Adults," *Journal of Marriage and Family* 64 (2002): 254–68.
28. Harsha N. Mookherjee, "Marital Status, Gender and Perception of 'Well Being,'" *The Journal of Social Psychology* (1997): 95–105.
29. Steven Stack and J. Ross Eshleman, "Marital Status and Happiness: A 17-Nation Study," *Journal of Marriage and Family* 60 (1998): 527–36.
30. Donald G. Dutton, "Patriarchy and Wife Assault: The Ecological Fallacy," *Violence and Victims* 9 (1994): 167–82; and Lisa K. Walder-Haugrud, Linda Vaden Gratch, and Brian Magruder, "Victimization and Perpetuation Rates of Violence in Gay and Lesbian Relationships: Gender Issues Explored," *Violence and Victims* 12 (1997): 173–84.
31. Jan E. Stets, "Cohabiting and Marital Aggression: The Role of Social Isolation," *Journal of Marriage and Family* 53 (1991): 669–80; Kersti Yllo and Murray Strauss, "Interpersonal Violence Among Married and Cohabiting

Couples," *Family Relations* 30 (1981): 339–47; and Jan E. Stets and Murray A. Strauss, "The Marriage License as a Hitting License: A Comparison of Assaults in Dating, Cohabiting, and Married Couples," paper presented at the 1988 meeting of the American Sociological Association, VB20F, pss, VB 119, 8 July 1988.

32. W. Bradford Wilcox and Steven L. Nock, "What's Love Got to Do with It? Equality, Equity, Commitment, and Women's Marital Equality," *Social Forces* 84 (March 2006).

33. Belinda Hewitt, Janeen Baxter, and Mark Western, "Family, Work, and Health: The Impact of Marriage, Parenthood, and Employment on Self-Reported Health of Australian Men and Women," *Journal of Sociology* 21 (March 2006): 61–78.

34. Alfred DeMaris and Catharine Kaukinen, "Violent Victimization and Women's Mental and Physical Health: Evidence from a National Sample," *Journal of Research in Crime and Delinquency* 42 (2005): 384–411.

35. Kei M. Nomaguchi, "Are There Race and Gender Differences in the Effect of Marital Dissolution on Depression?" *Race, Gender & Class* 12, no. 1 (2005): 11–30.

36. Walby, *Theorizing Patriarchy*, 201.

37. C. Owen Lovejoy, "The Origin of Man," *Science* 211 (January 1981): 348. Also: Ronald S. Immerman, "Perspectives on Human Attachment (Pair Bonding): Eve's Unique Legacy of a Canine Analogue," *Evolutionary Psychology* 1 (2003): 138–54.

10

The Curious Return of the Small Family Farm

In 1941, *The Prairie Farmer*, America's oldest farm periodical, celebrated its hundredth birthday. The centennial cover features a drawing of the iconic twentieth century "new" farmer: tall, young, and slender. Bulky overalls have given way to tailored city clothes; the straw hat to a fedora. In the artist's words, he is "a strong, virile, keen, friendly, forward-looking citizen standing in a field of gold."[1] Importantly, there are no horses or mules in that golden field. Instead, a tractor tills the ground. "Modern machinery has straightened the farmer's back," the artist happily reports. More boldly, an ad on the inside cover features a slender farm wife in stylish garb beaming over four small, happy children, with her husband on a tractor in the background. It declares that "[e]very new MM [Minneapolis-Moline] machine put into action on your farm brings you closer to FREEDOM, and closer to the young folks for whom you are farming."[2]

At that moment, American farmers and their families still numbered about twenty-nine million souls. The average farm was 160 acres in size.

The Prairie Farmer's cover for September 2007 features a photo of the occupational descendent of this archetypal industrial farmer. The twenty-first century farmer is fairly old, paunchy from lack of exercise, standing by his only son, and working 1,700 acres in corn. Indeed, driven by ethanol subsidies, "much of the countryside has been getting ready for bigger and bigger corn crops."[3] All the same, American farmers and their families now number about 4 million souls, a mere 14 percent of the 1941 figure, while the average farmer approached sixty years of age. Industrial agriculture had achieved its real end: not freedom and an abundance of children, but efficiency through the substitution of machines for people.

133

And yet, at this very apogee of the industrial farm, something new— and yet very old—seemed to be stirring within. Capitalistic farming appeared to be "pregnant": neither with some newly bioengineered chimera nor with the latest super-machine, but with a new *agrarianism*, a humanistic approach to agriculture that would reattach people to the soil. The farming future might not lie with the consolidators, specula- tors, and agribusinesses. Rather, it might rest upon the resurrection of a family-centered agriculture.

On the surface, this would seem to be perhaps the least feasible of twenty-first century possibilities. All the same, land-use expert Eric Freyfogle has enthused that "agrarianism is again on the rise" and that "agrarian ways and virtues are resurging in American culture."[4] Oddly, there is evidence to back up these claims.

The Household Restored

Poet, novelist, essayist, and farmer Wendell Berry labels agrarianism as the countervailing idea to industrialism. The industrial economy, he writes, is the culture of "the one-night stand. 'I had a good time,' says the industrial lover, 'but don't ask me my last name.'"[5] Agrarianism rests, in contrast, on a culture defined by marriage, a long-term covenant of mutual care. Brian Donahue underscores that it requires "that those who farm do so to fulfill their basic goal of a healthy family life on the land."[6] Lynn Miller, publisher and editor of *Small Farmer's Journal* (*SFJ*), says that agrarianism rests on two principles: "First, provide for the family [from the farm] and second, always be looking for ways to help family, friends, and neighbors."[7]

The key to building healthy agrarian households, Berry maintains, is recovering the tasks of both *husbandry* and *housewifery*. Husbandry is "the work of a domestic man, a man who has accepted a bondage to the household." The husbanding mind is "both careful and humble," ready "to keep, to save, to make last, to conserve." Under industrial agriculture, though, soil husbandry was displaced by a narrow "soil science"; animal husbandry, involving "the sympathy by which we recognize ourselves as fellow creatures of the animals," gave way to "animal science" and to "the animal factory which . . . is a vision of Hell." Even "the high and essential art of housewifery" surrendered at the universities to a "family and consumer science" that has blotted out the home.[8] Agrarianism means reinvigorating the household as "a center of economic productivity,"[9] restoring women and men to their natural and necessary tasks.

While sharing many traits, the new agrarianism differs from environmentalism in an important way. Particularly among "deep ecologists," human beings stand as the problem, the source of environmental degradation, a "cancer" on the planet. This view might be summarized as "the fewer humans, the better." In contrast, agrarians are buoyant humanists, welcoming children and the close settlement of human beings on the land. As two sympathetic writers summarize: "Agrarians . . . assert that a flourishing life standardly incorporates . . . interdependence with neighbors in a geographically limited, relatively self-sufficient, intergenerationally stable community; . . . and a measure of personal self-sufficiency through physical labor, preferably on one's own property."[10]

The Crisis of Industrial Agriculture

Contemporary agrarian writers underscore the weaknesses of industrialized farming. Foremost of these is the mounting inability of factory farms even to compete in a free market. Ohio's Gene Logsdon notes that in 1999, about half of the income that American farmers received came from the government, not farming. Put another way, "hardly any farmer in the Midwest is making a living from farming," relying instead on inheritances, other investments, state subsidies, and off-farm jobs to make ends meet.[11]

Meanwhile, farm operations grow ever more complex. "Rollover" deals for massive machines disguise actual ownership. "Custom sprayers apply all the fertilizers and pesticides. Hired 'scouts' watch for disease or insect infestations. Rented semi-trucks haul away the grain." Animal factories pump hogs and cattle full of hormones and antibiotics, leaving creatures that could not survive outdoors. Meanwhile, the actual "farmer" sits in an office before his computer, hunting for new tax loopholes and "hedging" on the Chicago Board of Trade.[12] Logsdon concludes that "this drift toward the total consolidation of power will collapse, because historically it has always collapsed. We are following unerringly in the footsteps of the old Roman Empire." More hopefully, on the ruins of agribusiness he sees emerging a fresh "landscape of garden farms."[13]

Economist John Ikerd focuses on confinement animal feeding operations (CAFOs) as the symbol of what is wrong in American agriculture. Promoted as economic development, and with the full backing of the agro-industrial establishment, these massive structures hold thousands of hogs, cattle, and other creatures in small stalls, animals never to touch real earth or smell fresh grass. "A CAFO is not a farm," Ikerd contends, "it is a factory. . . . [A]ll farms smell, but CAFOs stink." They also bring no improvements to their communities; usually relying on cheap immigrant labor, they create no jobs; and their unsightliness and odor drive off other economic opportunities. Ikerd notes that "corporations have no families, no communities, and increasingly no single nationality. Eventually, corporately controlled agriculture operations will be forced to leave rural communities in the U.S. and Canada."[14] Seeking cheaper labor, they will go to places like Brazil where, after another generation, they will probably die out.[15]

Berry acknowledges the intoxicating power of industrial agriculture. He recalls how, as a sixteen-year-old, he mowed a field with his father's new Farmall A tractor. Watching a nearby team of mules, "I remember how fiercely I resented their slowness." Indeed, he says that if you kept the context "narrow enough" and the accounting period "short enough," the industrial promises of higher productivity and the saving of labor made some sense. However, for the long run, the tractor also symbolized the shift from a farm economy largely resting on free solar power to one dependent on fossil fuels and a long supply line. "We had entered an era of limitlessness, or the illusion thereof, and this in itself is a sort of wonder." However, Berry insists that it cannot last: "the tirelessness of tractors brought a new depth of weariness into human experience, at a cost to health and family life that has not been fully accounted." As the prices of fossil fuels soar, as the costs of farm machinery become prohibitive, and as the machine-driven depopulation of the land nears its end, a deeper accounting grows necessary and the reality of limits returns. A new agriculture, resting on respect for these limits, is the only alternative.[16]

There are other signs of change at the macro-level, quietly and often indirectly summoning a new agrarianism. Miller suggests that the great rush to employ synthetic fuels will produce a "windfall" for oil crop farmers around the globe, "happy days for genetic engineering," and a consequent "accelerated environmental degradation and climate change." However, as more industrialized farm land is diverted to corn, soybeans, switchgrass, and oilseed, the demand for locally grown meat, vegetables, and feed will soar: "prices for all locally available farm commodities will go up, up, up." At the same time, the newly affluent Chinese "have discovered they have a taste for dairy products" just as "diet fashion" in North America has also shifted toward milk. This is generating new markets for small dairy operations. Indeed, as Miller writes, "a small independent family farm of limited but well-managed acreage could pull in an excess of 100,000 dollars per year in milk sales alone."[17]

In similar manner, diet fashion in North America is pushing toward the "'chic' organic equation." The demand for organics is actually doubling every three or four years. True, the predictable consolidation of retailers and producers is already occurring (e.g., Whole Foods buys out its chief rival). And yet, the small farmer is also reaping at least a "temporary" windfall: $10 and more for a gallon of organic raw milk; $5.50/lb for pasture raised chickens; fifty cents an egg; and $5/lb for organic vegetables. "Now all of a sudden many small independent organic farms are looking at profitable return of several thousand dollars per acre." Moreover, the clamor and degeneration of knowledge found on the World Wide Web are paralleled by new opportunities there for small farmers to make sales. Only partly with tongue in cheek, Miller declares that "there has never been a better time to be a farmer."[18]

A New Populism

Agrarian renewal can also be seen from the bottom up, as an expression of a new populism. Miller's *SFJ*, now in its fortieth year, serves about 20,000 subscribers. *SFJ* is a pleasing mix of practical articles on poultry raising, barn building, bee keeping, true horsepower, and market gardening, along with farm recipes, a kids' page, and reprints of rare and useful extension bureau booklets on pre-industrial farm techniques. Most enjoyable, though, are each issue's letters section that contains dozens of testimonials about building a new agrarian order, and—more surprisingly—the advertising section that showcases an array of mostly family-held businesses serving the new agrarians. Other sympathetic agrarian publications include *Touch the Soil, Farm and Life Newsletter, Countryside, Heavy Horse World* (from Britain), and *Back Home*.

Another bottom-up development has been the rapid spread of farmers' markets across the land. In 1994, there were 1,755 operating markets; in the year 2011, 6,000, an increase of 13 percent per annum and 250 percent overall. This form of direct marketing cuts out the notorious "middleman" in the food distribution process and encourages local production. About 30,000 American farmers now report selling their produce exclusively this way.[19]

A second form of direct marketing by farmers to consumers has emerged as well: Community Supported Agriculture (CSA). This method of linking producers to consumers and of insuring food quality had its origin in Germany, Switzerland, and Japan during the 1960s. The idea came to America in 1984, when Jan Vander Tuin of Switzerland teamed up with Robyn Van En of Great Barrington, Massachusetts, to create Indian Hill Farm. A CSA rests on an agreement between a farmer and a group of shareholders, who pay the cultivator a pre-negotiated fee in the late winter, in exchange for receipt of a box of produce every week from June through October. Under this shared "risk and reward" agreement, consumers eat what the farmer has successfully grown. CSAs differ from subscription farming in that the shareholders are guaranteed no particular quantity or type of food. Rather, they invest in the whole farm and receive what is seasonally ripe.

CSAs are also more of a "lifestyle" choice. Most feature organic or "biodynamic" produce, utilize heirloom varieties, employ apprentice and volunteer labor, hold work days and harvest festivals, and provide gift boxes of produce to needy households.

In the United States and Canada, the cost of a typical share ranges from $350 to $500; the size of CSAs vary from five to 1000 shareholders. The system provides the farmer with up-front capital and eliminates his marketing and weather risks. He can focus instead on the nurture of his crops and soil. Because distribution costs are low (boxes of produce usually go to a few distribution points), CSA produce is competitively priced. Recent estimates suggest that about 3000 CSAs now exist in North America. The largest is Angelic Organics in Boone County, Illinois, which is featured in the documentary film, "The Real Dirt on Farmer John."[20]

Another novel, bottom-up development is the emergence of grass farming as a viable form of agriculture. The movement is closely associated with geneticist Wes Jackson, who in 1976 founded the Land Institute in Salina, Kansas. Perhaps the ultimate reactionary, Jackson essentially believes that humankind has "been farming the wrong way for about 10,000 years." The Neolithic mistake came "when they started digging up the fields and baring the soil." Jackson sees the soil as a *non-renewable* resource, which should never feel a plow. He labels the earth "an ecological mosaic. We're only beginning to recognize the powers inherent in local adaptation." His is an agriculture based on perennial grasses, legumes, and sunflowers, together with grazing animals free of corn- and soybean-based feed. This is a "natural systems agriculture" that takes full advantage of the sun and seeks "a paradise of permanent pastures." Implementing this system in Ohio, Logsdon found after two years an astonishing vitality in his soil: "I began to understand why gatherings of graziers are so full of excitement compared to the sullen visages of farmers at grain conferences. We know that we are on to something revolutionary and hopeful."[21]

The new agrarianism also is in harmony with the New Urbanism, the populist rebellion against the drabness and sterile designs of suburbia. Most notably, the New Urbanists "share the agrarian's disdain for contemporary patterns of land use, taking inspiration instead from traditional modes." Put another way, both movements seek "renewal of traditions of human settlement that emerged over millennia." New Urbanists note that "human settlements have traditionally been oriented toward the pedestrian," and that "the neighborhood is the fundamental unit of human settlement." With keen insight, New Urbanists Benjamin Northrup and Bent Braxvoort Lipscomb note that a rural village "is essentially a single, free standing neighborhood in the country."[22]

Meanwhile, out in Exurbia, Logsdon welcomes a group he calls the "countrysiders." These are new refugees from the stress of urban and suburban life. They are the professionals and the telecommuters seeking "to bring back to rural America the life and money that consolidated banking sucked out over two centuries of predatory consolidation," a development then legitimized by consolidated schools. In a strong paragraph, he summarizes the aspirations of these new agrarians:

> We are rebelling against the economics of power. We want some income from the land but also some from nonfarm sources. . . . We want homes where our children can know meaningful work and learn something useful as they grow up. We want an alternative to chemicalized, hormonized, vaccinized, antibiotic-treated, irradiated factory food. We would like to establish home-based businesses . . . so that we do not have to put our children in day care centers. . . . Sometimes we homeschool our children.

These one foot in the country, one foot in the city "countrysiders" are working, he says, "to join the best of urban life with the best in rural life in a new and admirable agrarianism."[23]

An Intellectual Infrastructure

If ideas drive culture, and culture in turn drives politics, then the new agrarianism can also claim an impressive cadre of idea people, writers and scholars making the case. When Berry found his agrarian voice in the 1960s, he could identify allies only in the past: figures such as Liberty Hyde Bailey, founder of the Country Life Movement in 1919; or The Twelve Southerners noted before. However, by the 1970s a new community of writers began to gather around Berry. Early friends included Wes Jackson, Gene Logsdon, Hayden Caruth, poet Eric Trethewey, and the Ohio Amish farmer, editor, and author David Kline. A younger generation of writers and scholars has also rallied behind the agrarian banner. Seventeen doctoral dissertations alone have been written on Berry's work. In 2007, the University Press of Kentucky issued a fine *festschrift* entitled *Wendell Berry: Life and Work*, edited by Jason Peters and containing twenty-eight essays: they identify a new agrarian community of writers.

Berry notes that two failures have haunted the agrarian movement: the lack of a reliable accounting of industrialism's true effects; and the absence of a compelling agrarian economics.[24] Those gaps are also being filled by figures, such as Ikerd, now emeritus professor of agricultural economics at the University of Missouri. He began his career "as a conservative, bottom-line, free-market economist." However, his faith in the "invisible hand" was shaken by the farm crisis of the early 1980s, when even "good farmers" who did everything they were told by the experts went broke. He eventually concluded that this was not the inevitable consequence of agriculture, but rather the symptom of a distinctive type of farming; one "driven by specialization, standardization, and consolidation—an industrial agriculture driven by the economic bottom line."[25]

Ikerd continues to admire the classical economists—Adam Smith, David Ricardo, and Thomas Malthus—for having given as high a priority to "the social and ethical dimensions of life" as they gave to the economic. Smith, he says, also understood that *land* (and other natural resources) "constitutes 'by far' the greatest, the most important, and most durable part of the wealth of every extensive country." However, Ikerd breaks company with the "neo-classical" economists of the early twentieth century who, claiming to be true scientists, "abandoned the social and ethical foundations" of their predecessors.[26]

He goes on to explain why unfettered agro-capitalism will fail. He attributes this result to nothing less than the Second Law of Thermodynamics, or the Law of Entropy: the tendency of all closed systems to move toward the ultimate degradation of matter and energy. Life on earth, he writes, is only sustainable because of the daily flow of new solar energy into the system, which offsets entropy. For its part, capitalism "is a very efficient system of energy extraction," but its incentives provide scant encouragement to the use of solar power. In short, capitalism left to itself accelerates material entropy.

Ikerd insists, moreover, that capitalism also undermines social entropy. It weakens family and other personal bonds because maximum efficiency demands that people deal with each other impartially, or impersonally. Referring to the new globalist economy, he continues:

> Capitalist economies gain their efficient advantage by using people to do work, while doing nothing to restore the social capital needed to sustain positive personal relationships within society. There is no economic incentive for capitalists to invest in families, communities, or society for the benefit of future generations. And it is typically more profitable to find new people to exploit than to invest in education and training programs.

As the stocks of both material and social capital decline, Ikerd argues, the economy as a whole degenerates.

The result is the steady elimination of all boundaries, a motion toward sameness and uniformity. Ikerd notes that international capitalism works toward dissolving all political and cultural boundaries: trending to the creation of one world state and one global culture. Capitalist-driven entropy has the same effect on farming: "Tremendous gains in productivity and economic efficiency have been achieved by removing boundaries in agriculture to facilitate industrial production methods." For example, industrial farmers eagerly remove fences, or field boundaries, in order to introduce larger machines and to grow monocrops. The turn to animal factories is part of the same process. In short, "[r]ural landscapes have tended toward inert uniformity, without form, pattern, hierarchy, or differentiation."

From Ikerd's perspective, the only way to counter material entropy is to return agriculture to a reliance on the sun, not on fossil fuels and other extracted minerals. The only way to counter social entropy is to use culture and law to protect families, neighborhoods, and communities from intrusion by the incentives of capitalism.[27] And in fact, these might be called the central agrarian projects.

Troubles and Dilemmas

Still, the new agrarianism is not without its problems. To begin with, the current revival has its weird elements. Most of them cluster around the concept of "biodynamic" farming. This approach to agriculture counts Rudolf Steiner as its architect. Best known to Americans as the creator of Waldorf schools, Steiner (1861–1925) was an Austrian polymath; his collected works number 350 volumes. He called his over-all approach to life Anthroposophy. It stressed the unity of the spiritual and the sensory, the nature of the human being as body-soul-spirit, and his beliefs in reincarnation and the reality of the spirit world.

Near the end of his life, Steiner gave eight lectures to farmers near Breslau, Germany. They were published in 1924 as *Spiritual Foundations for the Renewal of Agriculture*. He maintained that a "farm is healthy only as much as it becomes an organism in itself—an indi-vidualized, diverse ecosystem guided by the farmer, standing in living interaction with the larger ecological, social, economic, and spiritual realities of which it is part."[28] Biodynamics can be distinguished from typical organic farming by practices designed "to achieve balance between the physical and higher non-physical realms; to acknowledge the influence of cosmic and terrestrial forces; and to enrich the farm, its products, and its inhabitants with life energy."[29] Central to biody-namic farming are nine "preparations" designed by Steiner to spur on composting or to be sprayed directly onto the soil or growing plants. For example, BD500 is made from cow manure fermented in a cow horn that has been buried in the soil during the autumn and winter. Other preparations employ yarrow and chamomile blossoms, stinging nettle, oak bark, and dandelions, all designed to enhance the "etheric" life forces on the farm. Biodynamic farmers also commonly plant, tend, and harvest their crops according to the sidereal lunar calendar.[30]

Going this far, biodynamic farming at the worst does no harm. At the best, these preparations do probably improve composting and overall soil health and the whole approach encourages close attention by the farmer to the vitality of his farm. One commentator even sug-gests that biodynamics represents "a renewal of the ancient peasants' culture."[31]

All the same, some biodynamic farmers have moved into clearly magical practices. "Dowsing" or "water witching," using a Y-shaped twig or L-shaped rod to locate water sources, sometimes appears on the biodynamic agenda. "Radionic" devices are also popular in the movement. They use a cup with knobs and dials, to which is added a sample of someone's blood, saliva, or urine. The devices allegedly mea-sure the "harmonics" and "Eloptic Energy" which define health, as they move through the human body. Radionic devices are also used to drive insects away from fields. In addition, a number of biodynamic farms employ the "Cosmic Pipe." Designed by T. Galen Hieronymous, it is said to "broadcast" through the soil the two "etheric forces" identified by Steiner: a downward flow focused on moisture and fertility; and an upward flow associated with dryness and ripening. These six-to-eight-foot tall cosmic conduits are constructed from PVC pipes and internally feature coils, reagent wells, and [of course] special crystals that concentrate the energy stream.[32] Some biodynamic farmers do worry that under these influences, "[w]e appear either pompous or kooky."[33]

A more serious problem is the argument that "[r]ealistically, few American families can return to the land as the primary center of the family economy." This assertion, articulated here by Freyfogle, also contends that the new agrarianism no longer "calls for widespread, equitable division of land." Few new agrarians, Freygogle says, urge land reforms that would divide large farms into small family homesteads or seek a new homestead act to encourage family settlement on public lands. He maintains that new agrarians "recognize that good farming requires highly specialized talents and is hardly an activity that the uninitiated can take up full-time with any prospect of success."[34]

In fact, some prominent agrarians do argue for a resettlement of the rural landscape (while admittedly often being short on specifics). Brian Donohue insists that "the task before agrarians is to make more agrarians." He even offers a vision of redistributed land: "Wouldn't it be nice if all of that eerily unsettled rural countryside were instead dense with diversified one-hundred-acre farmsteads, with their grain and hay rotations, livestock, and pastures embedded in a landscape of protected forest, wetland, and prairie?"[35] Berry agrees "that we need a farm population large, alert, and skilled enough, not just to make the land produce, but to take the best possible care of it as well."[36] Elsewhere, he adds that the longevity, coherence, and stability of human occupation "require that the land should be divided among many owners and users."[37]

I have (somewhat seriously) proposed a scheme that would divert existing federal crops subsidies for agribusinesses of $20 billion per annum into a fund supporting over one million new family farms. Recipients of settlement grants and loan guarantees would agree to maintain a family garden, practice simple animal husbandry, and open their farms to visiting school children. I conclude: "under my fantasy, we taxpayers would at least get what we thought we were paying for all along: a well-settled countryside of happy families and rosy-cheeked children."[38]

Creating "A Commons"?

The still larger problem here is land tenure. Donahue actually agrees with Freyfogle that a "golden age" of yeoman farming never existed in America. The former argues that American agriculture in the nineteenth century was "driven mainly by rapid extraction of natural capital [e.g., soil fertility] to supply distant markets." This was as true of the "Free Soil" Midwest as it was of the cotton-exporting South. He quotes Henry David Thoreau's mid-nineteenth century denunciation of American farming: "by avarice and selfishness, and a groveling habit . . . of regarding the soil as property, . . . the landscape is deformed, husbandry is degraded with us, and the farmer lives the meanest of lives."[39]

This problem is an old one and has frequently vexed agrarian dreamers. Simply put, a free market in agricultural land shows the same tendency of all unregulated markets toward consolidation. Over time, small family farms tend to disappear into larger holdings through death, inheritance issues, speculation, financial stress, property taxes, and a host of other pressures. Over a half century ago, European agrarians tackled the same question. In order to insure that "the land belong to those who till it," they concluded that the "value of land should not be determined by its market price." Instead, human labor should set "the standard of value."[40]

Some American new agrarians agree. Donahue openly breaks with the Jeffersonian tradition, arguing that a "widely dispersed private ownership of land by independent yeoman farmers" cannot be sustained. Indeed, he concludes that a "stable agrarian countryside cannot be founded solely on private farmers competing against one another to sell their produce for the lowest price."[41]

His favored solution is the creation of local and regional land trusts that would buy up the development rights to agricultural land. Farming families would still own "farming rights" to their land but would be prohibited from turning it to other uses. Corporations would also be prohibited from owning farmland. Forest lands would be owned outright by the trusts, forming a Commons. He recommends creation of a 1 to 2 percent tax on all real estate transactions to create these community trusts. Bonds to purchase development rights quickly could then be issued, guaranteed against the special tax.[42] Susan Witt of the E. F. Schumacher Society proposes an alternative where non-profit community land trusts would hold full title to crop land, which would then be returned to young farmers on ninety-nine-year leases. The latter would stipulate that the land must be farmed using organic procedures and that the farmer could pass the lease on to his heirs.[43] These schemes feed into a larger vision of a post-suburban American landscape, with "each township with its village of one or two thousand people concentrated onto a square mile or so, supporting the surrounding farms." Such villages scattered about the heartland would "have an agrarian sensibility, agrarian values, and above all, agrarian engagement."[44]

The dilemma is that the achievement of such a vision would require a very different mentality among Americans, a shift from the Jeffersonian dream (however problematic in practice) of freehold land to a more communitarian understanding of property. Donahue grasps the challenge here, explaining that "I am not demanding that corporate middle-managers surrender their backyards, shoulder their grubhoes, and march to the common fields for reeducation." Still, his vision of "towns in which private and common property rights flourish side by side" confronts formidable cultural barriers in America.[45] This may be the most problematic issue facing the new agrarians.

Old Dreams and New Prospects

Despite these problems, the American countryside is now in the early stages of ferment. Old dreams and ways, mixed with new tools, techniques, and opportunities, have given fresh life to the agrarian spirit. A way of living preserved through the twentieth century by sectarian religious groups such as the Old Order Amish has found new energy and new recruits in the opening years of the third millennium. The prospects for building a well-settled landscape of productive homes rich with the laughter of children seem more promising than has been the case for decades.

Notes

1. "Our Cover Page," *The Prairie Farmer* 113 (January 11, 1941): 3.
2. "Machinery Will Make Your Farm a Land of Freedom," *The Prairie Farmer* 113 (January 11, 1941): inside front cover. Caps in original.
3. Cherry Brieser Stout, "Get Ready for a Bin Buster," *Prairie Farmer* 179 (September 2007): cover, 6.
4. Eric T. Freyfogle, ed., *The New Agrarianism: Land, Culture, and the Community of Life* (Washington, DC: Island Press/Shearwater Books, 2001), xiii–xiv.
5. Wendell Berry, "The Whole Horse," in Freyfogle, *The New Agrarianism*, 64.

6. Brian Donahue, "The Resettling of America," in *The Essential Agrarian Reader: The Future of Culture, Community, and the Land,* ed. Norman Wirzba (Louisville: The University Press of Kentucky, 2003), 49.
7. Lynn Miller, "Inside the Circle," *Small Farmer's Journal* 31 (Summer 2007): 4.
8. Wendell Berry, *The Way of Ignorance and Other Essays* (Emeryville, CA: Shoemaker & Hoard, 2005), 96–100.
9. Freyfogle, *The New Agarianism,* xxxvii.
10. Benjamin E. Northrud and Benjamin J. Brukvoort Lipscomb, "Country and City," in *The Essential Agrarian Reader,* ed. Wirzba, 200.
11. Gene Logsdon, "What Comes Around," in *The New Agrarianism,* ed. Freyfogle, 82.
12. Gene Logsdon, *Living at Nature's Pace: Farming and the American Dream* (White River Junction, VT: Chelsea Green Publishing Company, 2000), 209–14.
13. Gene Logsdon, "All Flesh is Grass: A Hopeful Look at the Future of Agrarianism," in *The Essential Agrarian Reader,* ed. Wirzba, 155.
14. John Ikerd, "Reclaiming Rural America from Corporate America," a lecture for the Clean Water Network, Washington, DC, February 25, 2007; at http://web.missouri.edu/~ikerdj/papers/wash%20DC%20Reclaim.htm (8/9/2007): 2–4, 7.
15. Noted in Logsdon, "All Flesh is Grass," 166.
16. Berry, *The Way of Ignorance,* 93–96.
17. Miller, "Inside the Circle," 5.
18. Ibid., 4–5.
19. "Farmers Market Facts," at: http://www.ams.usda.gov/farmersmarkets/facts.htm (8/31/2007); and http://www.ams.usda.gov/farmersmarkets/FMstudystats.htm (8/31/2007).
20. Dan Imhoff, "Linking Tables to Farms," in *The New Agrarianism,* ed. Freyfogle, 19–26. Also: "Community-supported agriculture," at http://en.wikipedia.org/wiki/community-supported_agriculture (8/1/2007): 1–3.
21. Logsdon, "All Flesh in Grass," 168. Also: Wes Jackson, "The Agrarian Mind: Mere Nostalgia or a Practical Necessity," in *The Essential Agrarian Reader,* ed. Wirzba, 140–52; and Scott Russell Sanders, "Learning from the Prairie," in *The New Agarianism,* ed. Freyfogle, 5–13.
22. Northrup and Lipscomb, "Country and City," 191–99.
23. Logsdon, "What Comes Around," 87–89.
24. Berry, "The Whole Horse," 65.
25. Ikerd, "Reclaiming Rural America from Corporate America," 1.
26. John Ikerd, "Is Sustainable Capitalism Possible," lecture to The Life Economy Session of The World-Life Culture Forum-2006, Gyengong'gi Province, Republic of Korea, June 20–23, 2006; at http://web.missouri.edu/wikerdj.papers/korea%20-%20sustainable%20Capitalism.htm (8/9/2007): 10.
27. Ikerd, "Is Sustainable Capitalism Possible," 3–7, 10.
28. Rudolph Steiner, *Spiritual Foundations for the Renewal of Agriculture,* ed. M. Gardner (Junction City, OR: BioDynamic Farming and Gardening Association of the USA, 1993).

29. Steve Diver, *Biodynamic Farming and Compost Preparation* (Fayette, AR: Appropropriate Technology Transfer for Rural Areas, 1999), 2.

30. Diver, *Biodynamic Farming and Compost Preparation*, 3–4; and Walter Goldstein, "The Biodynamic Movement: Where Have We Been, Where Are We Going?" *Biodynamics* 232 (November/December 2000); at http://www. biodynamics.com/biodynamicsarticles/goldsteinbd.html (8/1/2007): 1–3.

31. Hilmar Moore, "Rudolf Steiner: A Biographical Introduction for Farmers," *Biodynamics* 214 (November/December 1997); at http://www.biodynamics. com/steiner.html (8/1/2007): 3.

32. See: Hugh Lovel, "Cosmic Pipe Workshop;" summary of a presentation at the East Coast Biodynamic Conference, October 5, 1997, in Shepherdstown, WV; at http://twelvestar.com/sourceworks/Cosmic%20Pipe%20Workshop. html (8/13/2007): 1–4.

33. Goldstein, "The Biodynamic Movement," 3.

34. Freyfogle, *The New Agrarianism*, xxix, xxxvii.

35. Donahue, "The Resettling of America," 49–50.

36. Berry, *The Way of Ignorance*, 119.

37. Berry, "The Whole Horse," 69.

38. Allan Carlson, "Agrarian Fairy Tales," *The Chesterton Review* 28, no. 3 (2002): 353–56.

39. In Donahue, "The Resettling of America," 40. Freyfogle's comment is found in *The New Agrarianism*, xxxv.

40. George M. Dimitrov, "Agrarianism," in *European Ideologies: A Survey of 20th Century Political Ideas*, ed. Felix Gross (New York: Philosophical Library, 1948), 414.

41. Donahue, "The Resettling of America," 38, 48.

42. Brian Donahue, "Reclaiming the Commons," in *The New Agrarianism*, ed. Freyfogle, 198–211.

43. Susan Witt, "New Agrarians," in *The Essential Agrarian Reader*, ed. Wirzba, 214–17.

44. Donahue, "The Resettling of America," 50.

45. Donahue, "Reclaiming the Commons," 211.

Index

DATE DUE